ACCOUNTING AND FINANCIAL SYSTEM REFORM IN A TRANSITION ECONOMY: A CASE STUDY OF RUSSIA

Accounting and Financial System Reform in a Transition Economy: A Case Study of Russia

Robert W. McGee
Andreas School of Business
Barry University
Miami Shores, Florida
USA

Galina G. Preobragenskaya
School of International Business
Omsk State University
Omsk, Russia

 Springer

Library of Congress Cataloging-in-Publication Data

Accounting and financial system reform in a transition economy: a case study of
    Russia / Robert W. McGee and Galina G. Preobragenskaya.

ISBN 0-387-23847-6   e-ISBN 0-387-23887-5   Printed on acid-free paper.

Printed in the United States of America.

9 8 7 6 5 4 3 2 1   SPIN 11349129

springeronline.com

TABLE OF CONTENTS

PREFACE

Much has been written about the economic and political problems of countries that are in the process of changing from centrally planned systems to market systems. Most studies have focused on the economic, legal, political and sociological problems these economies have had to face during the transition period. However, not much has been written about the dramatic changes that have to be made to the accounting system of a transition economy. This book was written to help fill that gap.

Using Russia as a case study we examined all the major aspects of accounting reform, starting with problems of implementation. We also examined the current state of auditing in Russia. Other studies looked at the changes in accounting education that are sweeping through Russian universities and the private sector and how international accounting certification is being used to meet the demand for credible accounting practitioners. We also devote chapters to corporate governance issues, the Russian tax system and the problems Russian enterprises face when they try to attract foreign direct investment.

We would like to thank the anonymous reviewers who made many helpful comments and suggestions to the early drafts of these papers and to the participants at the conferences where earlier drafts of these chapters were presented. Their comments and suggestions greatly improved the final product.

ACCOUNTING AND FINANCIAL SYSTEM REFORM IN A TRANSITION ECONOMY: A CASE STUDY OF RUSSIA

Chapter 1

INTRODUCTION

Accounting and financial system reform is not a new topic for Russian accountants and financial managers. Reform goes back to the days of the tsars. The communist revolution of 1917 produced additional changes, although the changes made to the accounting system were not nearly as drastic as the changes made to other aspects of the economy. Bookkeeping is basically bookkeeping. Debits continued to be on the left and credits on the right. There was no need for profit and loss statements, of course, since there were no profits and losses under communism. The inability to measure profits and losses, and thus the inability to efficiently allocate resources, was a structural deficiency in the socialist system, as Ludwig von Mises pointed out as early as 1920. The economic calculation debate focused on this very issue (Hayek 1935; Hoff 1981; Lange 1936, 1937; Lerner 1935; Lippincott 1938; Mises 1920, 1922, 1923, 1935; Polanyi 1923).

The reform process in Russia accelerated during the 1980s, especially after the Berlin Wall fell. After the dissolution of the Soviet Union, Russia and the other former Soviet republics realized that the accounting system they had was not adequate to meet the needs of a market economy. Although each of the former Soviet republics had the same accounting system at the start of the post-1989 reforms, changing from socialist accounting to market oriented accounting took different paths in different countries. This book tells the story of the reform in Russia.

Much of the information included in this book is based on interviews the authors conducted in Moscow, Saint Petersburg and a few other typical Russian cities, supplemented by the authors' experience gained by working in Russia and other former Soviet republics. Accounting practitioners from three of the Big-Four accounting firms were interviewed, as were accountants and auditors from several Russian firms. Accounting educators, certification specialists, tax specialists and corporate governance experts were also interviewed.

Much of the information gathered tended to confirm what was discussed in the existing literature. Thus, part of this book updates and expands on existing literature. However, new information was also uncovered that has not yet been discussed or addressed in the literature.

Most of the chapters in this book were first presented as conference papers, which improved the quality of the final product in several ways. When the various manuscripts were in the early draft stage a series of anonymous reviewers provided suggestions that led to improvements in subsequent drafts. Comments from participants at the conferences resulted in further changes.

This book examines not only accounting reforms but also other aspects of financial system reform, in the broad sense of that term. Issues relating to auditing, corporate governance, foreign direct investment, taxation and public finance, accounting education and accounting and finance certification are also discussed.

Chapter two examines the problems Russia faces in adopting and implementing International Financial Reporting Standards (IFRS), which many Russian companies are now required to follow. Part of the problem is that there is a lag between the time a new IFRS is issued in England and the time it is translated into Russian. Adoption is not automatic, which results in another time lag. Another problem is that Russia has not adopted all of the IFRS but only some of them. Furthermore, the standards that Russia adopts are not always a word for word equivalent of the standard that was issued in London, which leads unknowledgeable investors to place more confidence in the Russian version of IFRS than is warranted.

But that is not the end of the story. The Russian translation is less than perfect, many Russian accountants have not read either the Russian or English version of the standards, and many Russian accountants and managers do not see the need for IFRS. There is some justification for this viewpoint. Russian Accounting Standards (RAS) are also mandatory and accounting information prepared using RAS are the only documents that Russian tax officials are interested in viewing. Thus, there is a widespread perception that IFRS have no value, since they have a reading audience that is practically invisible. However, issuing financial statements based either on IFRS or U.S. GAAP is crucial for Russian companies that want to attract foreign capital, since international investors are neither knowledgeable about RAS nor interested in reading financial statements that have been prepared using them.

Chapter three discusses recent changes in Russian auditing. International Standards on Auditing (ISA) are in the process of being adopted and implemented but the process is far from complete. There is resistance to their adoption and there is less than a widespread perception that they are needed or desirable. Russian audit rules are not identical to ISA. Russia has some audit rules that are not part of ISA and the focus of audits at many Russian companies is tax compliance or minimization rather than attestation. Lack of full adoption and compliance with ISA makes it more difficult to attract international investment, since foreign investors do not place much confidence in financial statements that do not comply with IFRS and that were not audited using ISA.

Chapter four addresses issues of corporate governance, which is a new and rapidly changing field in Russia and other transition economies. Companies need good corporate governance practices not only to run efficiently but also to attract foreign investment. Yet present corporate governance practices leave much to be desired. Transparency and shareholder rights are relatively new concepts in Russia. Traditionally, there has been a tendency to hide relevant facts rather than disclose them. This view must change if Russian companies are to have good corporate governance practices.

Using internationally recognized financial reporting standards and adopting good corporate governance practices helps to attract foreign direct investment, which is the subject of chapter five. This chapter discusses foreign direct investment as it relates to Russia and other transition economies. Special attention is paid to the factors that international investors look at when determining where to invest. Several studies that examined various aspects of financial reporting and investment are also discussed.

Chapter six discusses the changes that Russia has had to make to its system of taxation and public finance as a result of shifting from a socialist economy, where all assets are owned by the government, to a market system where assets are owned privately. Funding government services during the early stages of the transition was a real problem, since there was no tax system in place to collect a portion of the income that was being generated in the private sector. New institutions and collection methods had to be created and implemented. This transformation still is not complete, although much progress has been made.

Chapter seven examines accounting education in Russian universities, which has greatly changed in recent years. A new generation of accountants has to learn IFRS and ISA and Russian universities have had to overcome some major problems in imparting this knowledge. Study materials were not always of the best quality. Sometimes learning materials did not exist. It has been difficult to find professors who have adequate knowledge of the new accounting rules and who are also willing to teach, since the market economy is enticing them away from the universities and into consulting. The rapid increase in the demand for accounting education, as evidenced by greatly increased enrollments in university accounting programs, has only served to exacerbate the problem, which still has not been completely solved.

Another rapidly changing area is that of certification of accounting and finance professionals. The Russian government has not moved forward in this area, which might be a good thing, since the market has rushed in to fill the void by supplying credible certification credentials much faster and perhaps better than the government would have been able to do. Various international groups that offer certification, such as the ACCA, the CMA and CFM and the CFA have started giving certification exams in Russian cities. The benefit of offering such certifications in Russia is that those who can pass the exams gain instant international credibility. The problem with the international certification exams is that most of them are given only in the English language, which prevents a large percentage of Russian accountants from participating or seeking these international certifications. This English-only problem is being addressed by a group that has started to offer international certification exams in the Russian language. However, these exams are in their infancy and have not yet become as widely recognized and accepted as their English-only counterparts.

The final chapter presents some concluding comments.

REFERENCES

Hayek, Friedrich A., editor. 1935. *Collectivist Economic Planning: Critical Studies on the Possibilities of Socialism.* London: George Routledge & Sons, Ltd., reprinted by Augustus M. Kelley Publishers, Clifton, NJ, 1975.

Hoff, Trygve J.B. 1981. *Economic Calculation in the Socialist Society.* Indianapolis: Liberty Press.

Lange, Oskar. 1937. On the Economic Theory of Socialism, II. *Review of Economic Studies* 4(2): 123-42.

Lange, Oskar. 1936. On the Economic Theory of Socialism, I. *Review of Economic Studies* 4(1): 53-71.

Lerner, Abba P. 1935. Economic Theory and Socialist Economy. *Review of Economic Studies* 2: 51-61.

Lippincott, Benjamin E., editor. 1938. *On the Economic Theory of Socialism.* Minneapolis: University of Minnesota Press.

Mises, Ludwig von. 1935. Economic Calculation in the Socialist Commonwealth, in Friedrich A. Hayek, editor, *Collectivist Economic Planning: Critical Studies on the Possibilities of Socialism*, pp. 87-130, London: George Routledge & Sons, Ltd., reprinted by Augustus M. Kelley Publishers, Clifton, NJ, 1975.

Mises, Ludwig von. 1923. Neue Beitrage zum Problem der sozialistischen Wirtschaftsrechnung [New Contributions to the Problem of Socialist Economic Calculation], *Archiv fur Sozialwissenschaft und Sozialpolitik* 51: 488-500.

Mises, Ludwig von. 1922. *Die Gemeinwirtschaft.* The second German edition (1932) was translated into English by J. Kahane and published as *Socialism: An Economic and Sociological Analysis* by Jonathan Cape, London, 1936. The full literary history of this book may be found in Bettina Bien Greaves and Robert W. McGee, compilers, *MISES: An Annotated Bibliography*, Irvington-on-Hudson, NY: Foundation for Economic Education, 1993 and also at www.mises.org.

Mises, Ludwig von. 1920. Die Wirtschaftsrechnung im Sozialistischen Gemeinwesen [Economic Calculation in the Socialist Commonwealth], *Archiv fur Sozialwissenschaft und Sozialpolitik* 47: 86-121.

Polanyi, Karl. 1923. Sozialistiche Rechnungslegung [Socialistic Accounting], *Archiv fur Sozialwissenschaft und Sozialpolitik* 49: 377-420.

Chapter 2

PROBLEMS OF IMPLEMENTING INTERNATIONAL FINANCIAL REPORTING STANDARDS IN A TRANSITION ECONOMY: A CASE STUDY OF RUSSIA[*]

Abstract

International Financial Reporting Standards (IFRS) and their predecessor, International Accounting Standards (IAS) are gaining in worldwide recognition. All publicly traded companies in the EU must adopt them by 2005 and many other countries either have adopted them or plan to do so in the near future. In 2002, the Russian Prime Minister announced that all Russian companies and banks must prepare their financial statements in accordance with international standards starting January 1, 2004. Implementing that decision will not be easy, for a variety of reasons. Not all international standards have been translated into Russian. Many Russian accountants are not sufficiently familiar with international standards to implement them. Some Russian universities have only recently started teaching international standards and the continuing education programs of the various Russian accounting associations are not yet prepared to offer comprehensive courses on international standards. Current Russian accounting standards conflict with international standards in several important ways and these conflicts will not be resolved in the near future.

This paper reviews the literature on this subject and incorporates the results of interviews conducted of Russian accounting firms, enterprises and university professors in July and August 2003.

---

[*] An earlier version of this paper was presented at the 8th International Conference on Global Business and Economic Development, Guadalajara, Mexico, January 7-10, 2004. Winner of the Best Paper Award.

INTRODUCTION

As transition economies go through the process of shedding their centrally planned accounting model and replacing it with a market oriented model that uses international standards they face a number of problems. Very few people know the new rules, since the international standards must first be translated into their language. Accountants who can read the international standards promulgated by the International Accounting Standards Board and its predecessor, the International Accounting Standards Committee in the original English have a competitive advantage in this regard, but trying to fully exploit this advantage may be frustrating if potential clients or employers do not place much value on international standards.

There is also an inertia barrier to overcome. It is difficult to change the status quo (Friedman & Friedman 1984). Accountants and managers who have been using the old system for 20 or 30 years do not want to change because they feel comfortable with the system they learned in school or on the job when they were young. Those individuals also happen to be the people who are now in charge of enterprises and accounting departments, so their approval must be had before any new system can be adopted and implemented.

A number of countries that have started this conversion process have experienced similar problems. No one knows the new rules but there is nowhere to go to take classes to learn the new rules because no one can be found to teach the new knowledge. Most universities do not have qualified professors and most accounting firms do not have anyone who has been trained in the new rules. Yet the governments in these countries often pass laws with deadlines, stating that the new rules must be adopted by some certain date.

What results when this happens is that the new rules cannot be implemented according to the government's schedule because nobody knows how to implement them. A new set of problems result from this top-down approach to accounting reform. Various ways have been tried to alleviate or solve the problems that result from adopting new accounting rules. Some have worked better than others. This paper examines the Russian case, which is still in the process of transformation.

REVIEW OF THE LITERATURE

Much has been written about International Accounting Standards (IAS), International Standards on Auditing (ISA), accounting harmonization, accounting education and accounting reform in transition economies in recent years. A few books and articles have focused on accounting reform in Russia.

The classic book in the sub field of accounting reform in Russia is by Enthoven et al (1998). This book discusses the Russian accounting system, management accounting, auditing, taxation and accounting education. A few years before that, Enthoven et al (1992) published a book on doing business in Russia and other former Soviet republics that dealt with accounting issues. This latter book was very popular among accounting practitioners who were doing business in the former Soviet Union, since it was one of the few major sources of accounting information on Russia at the time it was published.

Bailey (1982) published a long historical study of Russian accounting going back to the thirteenth century. Shama and McMahan (1990) discuss the historical development of accounting in Russia from Tsarist times to communism and also how perestroika will change the nature of accounting in Russia and other East European countries. Motyka (1990) discusses the impact of Western Europe on accounting development in tsarist Russia prior to 1800. Lebow and Tondkar (1986) discuss the development of accounting in the Soviet Union and its effectiveness. Two decades before that, Campbell (1963) published a book containing a series of essays on Soviet accounting problems. Campbell (1956) also did a long and detailed study of depreciation under the Soviet accounting system. Horwitz (1963) discusses some of the philosophical and historical literature on accounting in a socialist regime and focuses his attention on depreciation and cost.

An early study by Mills and Brown (1966) discusses how shifting from a production model to a profitability accounting model would help Soviet enterprise managers make decisions that would increase the efficiency of their firms and help them to better allocate resources. In a similar vein, Thornton (1983) discusses changes in the way the Soviets accounted for factor costs over a twenty-five year period. A study by Scott (1969) states that Soviet accounting after the 1965 reforms started to place more emphasis on enterprise profitability, which helped move the Soviet economy closer to a Western market model.

Other authors have also touched on this theme. Horwitz (1970) discussed the effect that decentralization has on the management accounting control system. Chastain (1982) described how the Soviet accounting system was not able to keep up with the needs of enterprise managers. He also assesses the implications of that inability for the accounting profession.

Gorlick has done several studies on the Soviet accounting system. In one study he discusses the historical development and problems of uniform accounting (1974a). In another he discusses planning and control (1974b). In an earlier study he discussed the difference in accounting measurements between the Soviet Union and the United States and the advantages and disadvantages of their profitability measurements (1971).

Richard (1998) wrote a book chapter that discussed communist accounting systems in Eastern Europe in general and in the Soviet Union in particular. Garrod and McLeay (1996) edited a book on accounting in transition economies, which provides a good introduction to many of the issues involved in attempting to convert the accounting system from a central planning model to a market model. One of the chapters in that book (Jaruga 1996) describes the changing accounting function in socialist countries, which is now mainly of historical interest.

Turk and Garrod (1996) discuss the lessons Slovenia learned when it began the process of changing to International Accounting Standards. The Slovenian experience is not unlike the Russian experience in many ways. Preobragenskaya and McGee did research on the relationship between IAS and foreign direct investment (FDI) in Russia (2003a) and on the state of auditing in Russia (2003b). Their FDI study concluded that the lack of credibility of Russian financial statements was hampering inflows of foreign capital. Their audit study found that the state of auditing in Russia is not yet up to western standards.

A few studies have been made on accounting education in Eastern Europe or the former Soviet Union. According to one scholar, Houghton Mifflin's 1300-page Principles of Accounting was the first Western accounting text sold in the Soviet Union (Collingwood 1991). It was translated and distributed by Finansy I Statistika, Moscow's government owned publisher. Kobrack and Feldman (1991) speculated whether the reform process in the Soviet economy could create a new market for accounting textbooks. McGee has written about educating accounting professors in Bosnia & Herzegovina (2003a) and reforming accounting education in Armenia (2003b).

There are several sources of information on recent developments in accounting reform in Russia. The International Center for Accounting Reform in Moscow [www.icar.ru/] publishes the *ICAR Newsletter*. The World Bank publishes *Transition Newsletter*, which gives current information about various aspects of market reforms in transition economies, including accounting reform in Russia. The Russian websites of the Big-Four accounting firms also have current information and, in some cases, publications.

The Deloitte & Touche Russian website has an e-library link that contains a variety of items on various aspects of doing business in Russia. It has a *Doing Business in Russia Online Guide*, which includes much information on accounting and tax topics. It has several newsletters that address accounting, tax and legislative issues on various countries, including Russia. *Russia - Legislative News* is a monthly newsletter that contains accounting and tax items. Legislative Tracking is a daily publication that keeps readers abreast of Russian pending legislation.

Ernst & Young publishes *An EYe on Russia*, a monthly newsletter on current business, accounting and tax issues. It also has a Russian Legislation website that contains downloadable documents on Russian accounting, tax and related legislation that have been translated into English.

The KPMG Russian website has several good publications, including *Doing Business in Russia* and *Russia – Tax Overview*. It also has the GAAP 2001 and 2002 studies.

The PricewaterhouseCoopers website has several publications pertaining to Russia, including *Doing Business in the Russian Federation* (2003). There are also a number of short articles by PWC partners and others on various aspects of accounting reform in Russia, including an excellent article by Leonid Schneidman (2003) on the long road to IAS adoption. The PWC site also has the GAAP reports for 2002, 2001 and 2000 available for downloading in several languages.

Some publications have compared the accounting standards in various countries to IAS. The most thorough study is GAAP 2001, a joint publication of several large international accounting firms, which makes comparisons for 62 countries, including Russia. Several of the Big-Four accounting firm websites have a link to this study. The International Forum of Accountancy Development website [www.ifad.net] has published this study in interactive format. There is also a *GAAP Comparison 2000* study that provides comparisons for 52 countries and a small 2002 update titled *GAAP 2002 Convergence* that provides data on 59 countries. Street (2002) has written a summary of the GAAP 2001 study.

The internet also has information on corporate governance in Russia. One good source is the Independent Directors Association website, which contains much up to date information on corporate governance in Russia. It publishes *Independent Director*, a quarterly review and has also published *The Code of Conduct of Independent Directors* and *The Independent Directors Association Charter*, both of which are published in the Spring 2003 issue. The Organisation for Economic Cooperation and Development (OECD) website also has current and relevant information on corporate governance in Russia. *The Russian Code of Corporate Conduct* can be accessed from several websites, including the Deloitte & Touche Russian website. The Corporate Governance Code can be obtained from the Russian Institute of Directors website [www.rid.ru].

METHODOLOGY

The first stage in the preparation of this paper was a thorough review of the literature on accounting reform in general and accounting reform in Russia and other transition economies in particular, with special attention being paid to the literature that discussed the adoption and implementation of IFRS. As the literature was being reviewed, the authors started compiling a tentative list of questions to ask Russian accounting experts on various aspects of accounting reform in Russia. This list was sent to the individuals to be interviewed several weeks prior to the interviews.

After the list of questions was compiled, the next step was to identify and contact individuals who were experts in some aspect of the present state of Russian accounting, which was done through a combination of website searches, telephone calls in both Russia and the United States and e-mail communications. It was difficult to contact some individuals, especially at Russian universities, because they were away on summer holiday. However, a sufficient number of experts with diverse backgrounds on various aspects of accounting reform in Russia were able to be contacted and interviewed to make the project worthwhile. Once experts were identified, initial contact was made and interviews were scheduled. On-site interviews took place during July and August 2003 in St. Petersburg, Moscow and Omsk. Telephone interviews were also conducted with individuals located in Washington, DC and Geneva, Switzerland. Individuals from the following institutions participated in the on-site interviews:

Deloitte & Touche, Moscow office [www.deloitte.ru]
KPMG, Moscow office [www.kpmg.ru]
KPMG, St. Petersburg office [www.kpmg.ru]
PricewaterhouseCoopers, Moscow office [www.pwcglobal.com/ru]
Ajour, a Russian auditing and consulting firm, Moscow [www.ajour.ru]
PKF (MKD), a Russian audit and consulting firm, St. Petersburg office
    [www.mcd-pkf.com]
Independent Directors Association, Moscow
[www.independentdirector.ru]
MDM Group, Moscow [www.mdmgroup.ru]
St. Petersburg State Polytechnical University [www.spbstu.ru]
St. Petersburg State Railway University (a.k.a. Petersburg State
    Transport University) [www.pgups.ru]
Timiryazev Agricultural Academy, Moscow [www.timacad.ru]
Hock Accountancy Training, Moscow office [www.hocktraining.com]
Omsk State University [www.omsu.omskreg.ru]
Omsk State Institute of Service
[www.omsk.net.ru/education/vuz/service/main.htm]

The information gathered from these interviews was combined with information that was already published and available. While much of the information gathered during the course of the interviews confirmed what the existing literature already said, much new information was gathered that filled in the gaps in the existing literature and extended and updated prior studies in several important ways.

PROBLEMS OF IMPLEMENTING INTERNATIONAL STANDARDS

Accounting in Russia

Accounting has a long history in Russia (Bailey 1982; Shama and McMahan 1990), going back at least to the thirteenth century, through the time of the tsars and through the communist era. The Russian accounting system started shifting away from the centrally planned, socialist model as early as the 1960s (Mills and Brown 1966; Scott 1969; Jaruga 1996; Thornton 1983). The pace accelerated with perestroika and the collapse of the Soviet Union, which began in the late 1980s. A critical year for Russian accounting was 1989. It was in that year that the Soviet government introduced legislation for joint ventures using foreign capital. This decision created a real need to modify the Russian accounting system and led to the introduction of new Western accounting concepts like audits, intangible assets, capital, etc.

Some scholars have gone on record as saying the reason for the collapse of the Soviet Union was because of the inability to allocate resources efficiently under a socialist accounting system (Sennholz 2002; Rothbard 1991). Ludwig von Mises, an Austrian scholar who later taught at New York University, predicted the collapse as early as the 1920s (Mises 1920; 1922; 1923; 1935). His prediction sparked the socialist calculation debate of the 1930s (Hayek 1935; Lange 1936; 1937; Lerner 1935; Lippincott 1938; Hoff 1981). Polanyi (1923) agreed with Mises that the problem of economic calculation is insoluble in a centrally planned economy but proposed to solve the problem by means of "a functionally organized socialist transition-economy."

Whatever the reason(s) for the collapse of the Soviet Union, there has been a worldwide movement on the part of formerly centrally planned economies to move away from the top-down, centrally planned accounting model and toward a bottom-up market model. Russia started to make the transition by deciding to adopt and implement international standards. Although Russia chose to adopt and implement international standards several years ago, there are still some glitches in the system.

Until recently, deducting the cost of an IAS audit was not allowed by the Russian tax code (Ermakova 2003), which took some of the incentive away from having such an audit. Russian accountants and auditors are not sufficiently well versed in international standards to implement them, with a few exceptions. There is a widespread perception on the part of accountants who work for the large international accounting firms that none of the Russian accounting firms, even the biggest ones, are able to provide high quality service regarding international standards. The large international accounting firms, mostly the Big-Four, have rushed in to fill the gap to provide the services and expertise that the local Russian firms cannot provide. This capturing of market share by the big firms has caused some resentment on the part of the smaller Russian firms. It has also given some Russian accounting firms an inferiority complex, since they know they do not have the resources or expertise to compete against the international firms. Russian accounting firms have lost some large clients to the Big-Four. However, some of their big clients later returned, partly because of cost considerations.

Russian accountants and auditors who were trained under the old system need to learn the new system and many of them have not. Some of them, especially the older ones, are actively resisting the change. Some Russian accountants and professors, even at the top, insist that they use or teach international standards, even though they have never read them. There is the widespread perception that Russian Accounting Standards (RAS) either are the same as the international standards or are just as good. In fact, there are major differences. RAS are more form over substance, whereas the international standards are more substance over form.

There is also the perception that international standards are not needed, either because the RAS are just as good as the international standards or because there is no demand for international standards. There is a grain of truth to the lack of demand argument. Until a few years ago, the only reason most firms prepared financial statements was to provide information to the tax authorities. Some firms still prepare financial statements just for the tax authorities. However, the trend now is away from having a monopsony (single user) of accounting information, especially with the large Russian firms, since they need to go to the international capital markets for funds to expand or stay afloat. Foreign investors demand to see financial statements prepared using either IFRS or U.S. GAAP as a condition of talking seriously about investing in a Russian company.

It would not be an overstatement to say that companies prepare statements using either IFRS or U.S. GAAP only because they need to in order to obtain a listing on some foreign stock exchange or because their creditors or investors demand it. The demand for such statements is therefore limited, especially when companies prepare such statements at the consolidated level. It is typical that subsidiaries prepare statements based on RAS and that GAAP adjustments are made at the top, even though the people who provide the information used for consolidation are further down the organization and know nothing about GAAP principles. Top corporate managers seldom use consolidated information for management decision making purposes, since such information has no value to them. This valuelessness of IFRS or U.S. GAAP consolidated financial statements is especially true for tax managers, since they use only the RAS statements for computing the company's tax liability.

Although the trend is to place more emphasis on the needs of shareholders and potential investors and less on the needs of tax authorities, not all Russian accountants and managers feel this way. Most accountants who work for the big international accounting firms, and many of their clients, now recognize the goal of financial statements is to provide information to shareholders, not the tax authorities. This change in attitude and perception started to take place around 1999 or 2000.

This change in attitude has not yet filtered down to the smaller firms and enterprises. Although the big accounting firms and an increasing number of large enterprises now recognize that the main audience for the financial statements they prepare are shareholders, the smaller Russian companies still think that accounting information is only for the tax authorities. Some CEOs at larger companies still think this way.

This attitude is reinforced by the Russian tax authorities themselves, who often could not care less to see any financial statements based on international standards. The Russian tax rules are different from IFRS, so why bother to look at financial statements that are prepared using IFRS? They want to look only at statements prepared using RAS. One of the partners interviewed at one of the international accounting firms said he was tired of having to sign off on two sets of financial statements, one based on RAS and one based on either IFRS or U.S. GAAP. He longed for the day when he would need to sign off on only one set of statements. He also confided that such a day is likely far off, since statutory accounting still requires the use of RAS and this rule is unlikely to change any time soon.

Not all Russian enterprises that are trying to attract foreign capital are using IFRS. Some of them are using U.S. GAAP. One of the deciding factors that enters into the decision to use one or the other set of internationally recognized financial reporting standards has to do with which capital market the enterprise wants to tap into. If they are targeting the United States capital market, they often decide to use U.S. GAAP. Those who decide to tap into the European capital market often choose IFRS. Russian enterprises used to prefer U.S. GAAP to IFRS because they wanted to list their shares in New York. The trend is now toward IFRS because of the Enron and Arthur Andersen scandals. However, not all firms are shifting to IFRS. The subsidiaries of the many U.S. firms in Russia prefer GAAP, so it appears that there will be a need for GAAP-trained accountants for the foreseeable future.

The interviews revealed that there is a bit of standards shopping going on on the part of some Russian enterprises. In one case, an enterprise would have had a multimillion deferred tax liability using one set of standards, whereas their tax liability using the other set of standards would have been zero. One set of rules would have treated the book tax difference as a permanent difference whereas the other standards would have treated the difference as a timing difference, and thus subject to deferral. Not surprisingly, the enterprise chose to use the set of standards that did not result in a tax liability.

Some Russian audit firms will agree to sign anything, including an audit report, lest they lose a client. Or at least that is the perception. Unfortunately, there may be some truth to this perception. Russian business culture is different than Western business culture in this respect. Three generations of communist governments and the accompanying corruption that went with it have made people cynical. Many people simply do not believe that financial statements signed by a Russian audit firm are as credible as statements signed by a Western audit firm (Rozhnova 2000).

One solution to this dilemma would be to establish a strong private sector accounting organization like the American Institute of Certified Public Accountants (AICPA) or one of its British counterparts that is capable of policing its members and giving much needed moral support to the Russian audit firms that do not want to give into the pressure to sign audit opinions when financial statements are not of sufficiently high quality. This solution was proposed both by the Russian firms that were interviewed and by some members of the Big-Four. Unfortunately, no such private sector accounting organization currently exists and none are on the horizon. There are a number of small, politically weak accounting organizations, but they do not have the authority, power or incentive to do the policing job or to provide the moral authority needed to support the honest Russian audit firms that want to do the right thing.

It is encouraging that Russian accountants have identified the problem and have a good idea of where the solution might lie. The next step is to find a way to achieve the desired result. That will not be easy, at least for the immediate future, since the Russian accounting profession, in the Western sense of that term, is in its infancy stage. There is no recent history of private sector institution building in Russia and the other former communist countries. The only institution was the State, and in some cases, the church. Private sector institutions will need to be created and grow in size and strength, and that process will take time, perhaps a generation or more. One individual from a Big-4 accounting firm expressed pessimism about the possibility of a strong and independent accounting association coming into existence in the near future. He did not think it was realistic to expect such an independent organization to be established and function in Russia because it is against the Russian management culture to have such organizations.

Some of the individuals interviewed pointed out that part of the problem is that the professional accounting organizations that do exist have a bias in favor of the status quo. So do Russian bureaucrats. Milton Friedman discussed this inertia problem in theoretical terms several years ago

(Friedman and Friedman 1984). One of the interviewees said that these people do not know anything about international standards, that they do not have the required skills and that changing to international standards could put them out of a job.

Outside help is available for strengthening these private sector accounting associations. George Soros and his various foundations have recognized the need to build and strengthen private institutions and have allocated millions of dollars toward this goal. The various USAID and Tacis accounting reform projects include an institution building component in their projects. The problem with some of these institution building projects is that they turn out to be top-down. The local accountants and existing accounting organizations need to be convinced that they need to build such institutions. The institution building process would go faster and smoother and would be more successful if the process were demand driven, with the demand emanating from the grass roots rather than from some international organization that offers to drop money and consultants on the problem.

Another structural problem with Russian accounting is the Russian mindset. Under the old centrally planned system, accountants were really bookkeepers. They didn't have to make decisions. Their job was just to make journal entries. There was no such thing as exercising professional judgment. Where a decision had to be made, their solution was to look for some rule that told them what to do. The new rules, whether IFRS or GAAP, require the exercise of professional judgment and many Russian accountants do not feel comfortable making decisions on their own. They would prefer to find some rule in a book that instructs them on how to do everything and they resist adopting the new rules. This structural bump in the road to the adoption and implementation of market based accounting rules will be worn down with time, but it will take perhaps a generation or more before Russian accountants think the same way as Western accountants in regard to this approach to decision making.

Several government ministries are involved in accounting reform. Unfortunately, they do not always think the same way. In fact, their approaches to accounting reform are drastically different. The Ministry of Economic Development and Trade is strong on policy formation but does not have much power over policy implementation. Its approach is bottom-up. The Finance Ministry, on the other hand, prefers a top-down approach, similar in structure to the old centrally planned Soviet system. Westerners feel more comfortable dealing with the Ministry of Economic Development and Trade, since Western accountants also prefer a bottom-up approach.

However, these two ministries are not the only government agencies that are involved in accounting reform. The Russian Securities Commission and the Central Bank also play a role. In 2002 the Association of Russian Entrepreneurs also became involved in accounting reform. But no one is in charge. There is no leadership. There is no central direction to accounting reform. It is almost like all of these institutions are groping in the dark. While some government ministries demonstrate an interest in accounting reform, they are unable to answer questions because of a lack of expertise.

There is no force driving accounting reform, from an organizational perspective. No organization wants to protect both accounting and the public interest. The pressure to reform accounting in Russia is coming from the market. Russian enterprises that want to raise capital, either by debt or equity financing, need to have statements prepared either according to IFRS or GAAP. Potential investors demand it. That is the factor that is causing the change, not some government bureaucracy that dictates policy and rules from on high.

Most of the largest companies, like Gasprom, Aeroflot, metallurgical plants, electricity plants, etc., including 80 percent of the biggest companies and 95 percent of banks prepare financial statements based either on IFRS or U.S. GAAP. The real driver of accounting reform is the large companies. They are doing it in spite of government inaction. The market is solving the problem without government.

International Standards in Russia

Accounting is part of the legislative system. That is a problem because Russia will never have true international standards if government has to legislate it. There will always be a lag and style and language problems. The original plan by the Russian Finance Ministry in 1998 was to adopt all IAS by 2000. That did not happen. The new target for full adoption and implementation was 2004, at least in the case of banks and publicly traded companies. However, that target is also has not been met. In fact, not a single accountant interviewed thought that international standards would be fully adopted and implemented by 2004. One accountant estimated that full implementation would take ten years.

Even though Russia is in the process of adopting international standards, it has not adopted all of the international accounting standards, and it has no immediate plans to adopt the standards it has not already adopted. It has not adopted the standards on impairment, financial instruments or hyperinflation. There are good reasons for not adopting each of these standards.

In the case of the standard on impairment, many Russian companies and their accountants do not want to apply the impairment rules because many companies have assets that are overvalued. Applying the impairment standard would cause the asset side of the balance sheet to shrink, considerably in many cases, and they do not want that to happen. In extreme cases, a company that appears healthy could appear to be insolvent if the impairment rules were applied. This hesitancy is not unique to Russia. The same situation exists in Republika Srpska, the Serbian part of Bosnia, and in other formerly centrally planned economies.

Perhaps the main reason why the standard on financial instruments has not been adopted is lack of demand. Very few Russian enterprises use complex financial instruments, and the ones that do are already applying the IFRS or U.S. GAAP on this topic. Also, this standard is difficult to understand and many Russian accountants are not eager to make the effort to learn a standard that they probably will not use in the foreseeable future.

The standard on hyperinflation is not needed, or at least that is the perception of many Russian accountants, because Russia's inflation rate has fallen below the threshold needed to trigger the hyperinflation standard. Russia's cumulative inflation over the most recent three years (2001-2003) has been about 90 percent, and the threshold for using the hyperinflation standard is 100 percent. But the 100 percent test is only one of five items on the IFRS list of possibilities. To be more compliant with IFRS it is necessary to look not only at quantitative factors but also qualitative factors. For example, Russian companies do their planning in dollars, not rubles. If the ruble is not being used to make management decisions, a strong argument can be made that the hyperinflation accounting rules should be used even if the inflation rate does not hit the 100 percent minimum threshold.

Another point that could be made about Russia's adoption of international standards is that even the standards that have been adopted may not always be international standards. For example, the Russian standard on income taxes is based on the old version of the IAS income tax standard, not the new one. This fact is known within much of the Russian accounting community but may not be as well known outside of Russia. Another, less well known fact about Russia's accounting standards is that the Russian version of the standards that have been adopted are not mere translations of the English language originals. In many cases they are abbreviated, simplified versions of the original English language IAS. RAS tend to be much shorter, more detailed and conceptual. They cover a fraction of the content of IAS. In short, it may not be accurate to state that Russia has adopted IFRS. It would be more descriptive to say that Russian accounting standards are merely based on IFRS. Often the differences between RAS and IFRS are not large or important. However, the difference may be substantial, such as in the area of accruals principles.

Many studies have been made that compare RAS to IAS, or that list the Russian accounting standards that are on the same topics as the IAS. The GAAP 2000 and GAAP 2001 studies are perhaps the most famous and most accessible, since they were done by reputable firms and since they are available on the internet in several languages. PricewaterhouseCoopers updated the GAAP 2001 study in its *Doing Business in the Russian Federation* publication (2003). A summary of that update is shown in Table 1. This table compares the rules that were in force on March 15, 2003.

Table 1
Differences between Russian Accounting Standards and International Accounting Standards

Russian accounting may differ from that required by IAS because of the absence of specific Russian rules on recognition and measurement in the following areas:	
- the classification of business combinations between acquisitions and unitings of interest	IAS 22.8
- provisions in the context of business combinations accounted for as acquisitions	IAS 22.31
- consolidation of special purpose entities	SIC 12
- the restatement of financial statements of a company reporting in the currency of a hyperinflationary economy in terms of the measuring unit current as of the balance sheet date	IAS 29.8
- the translation of the financial statements of hyperinflationary subsidiaries	IAS 21.36
- the treatment of accumulated deferred exchange differences on disposal of a foreign entity	IAS 21.37
- derecognition of financial assets	IAS 39.35
- the recognition of operating lease incentives	IAS 17.25; SIC 15
- accounting for defined benefit pension plans and some other types of employee benefits	IAS 19.52
- accounting for an issuer's financial instruments	IAS 32.18/23
- hedge accounting for derivatives	IAS 39.142
- the treatment of exchange differences resulting from severe devaluation or depreciation of a currency	IAS 21.21; SIC 11
There are no specific rules requiring disclosures of:	
- a primary statement of changes in equity	IAS 1.7
- a primary statement of cash flows; and the notion and definition of cash equivalents, and detailed guidance on the preparation of cash flow statements	IAS 7
- the FIFO or current cost of inventories valued on a LIFO basis	IAS 2.36
- the fair values of financial assets and liabilities	IAS 32.77
- the fair values of investment properties	IAS 40.69
- related parties information except by certain reporting companies with a specific legal form (joint stock companies); the definition of a related party is a narrower one, based on legislation	IAS 24.1-4
- certain segment information (e.g. a reconciliation between the information by reportable segment and the aggregated information in financial statements, significant non-cash expenses, other than depreciation and amortization, that were included in segment expense and, therefore, deducted in measuring segment result – for each reportable segment)	IAS 14.61/67

There are inconsistencies between Russian rules and IAS that could lead to differences for many enterprises in certain areas. Under Russian rules:	
- goodwill is calculated by reference to the book values of acquired net assets	IAS 22.40
- proportionate consolidation may be used for subsidiaries in which the parent has 50 percent or less of the voting power	IAS 27.15
- revaluation of property, plant and equipment is allowed but gives different results than IAS and need not be kept up-to-date	IAS 16.29
- the useful life of property, plant and equipment is usually determined using periods prescribed by the government for tax purposes, which are longer than those for which the assets are expected to be used, but in practice the management of a company sets the periods in the accounting policy	IAS 16.6/41
- if investment properties are revalued, they are still depreciated	IAS 40.27
- if investment properties are revalued, the gains and losses are not required to be taken to the income statement	IAS 40.28
- finance leases are generally defined in legal terms and the right of capitalization is given to a lessor or a lessee by the Contract	IAS 17.3/12.28
- lessors recognize finance lease income differently	IAS 17.30
- the completed contract method can be used for the recognition of revenues on construction contracts when the outcome of a construction contract can be estimated reliably	IAS 11.22
- trading, available-for-sale and derivative financial assets are not recognized at fair value	IAS 39.69
- trading and derivative liabilities are not recognized at fair value	IAS 39.93
- any financial investments are not required to be carried at fair value	IAS 39
- provisions can be established more widely or less widely than under IAS, and there is no requirement for discounting	IAS 37.14/45
- own (treasury) shares are shown as assets	SIC 16
- classification of cash flows between investing and financing activities in the cash flow statement may be different from IAS	IAS 7.6/16/17
- cash flow statements reconcile to cash rather than to cash and cash equivalents	IAS 7.45
- the correction of fundamental errors is included in the determination of the net profit or loss for the reporting period, but separate disclosure and pro-forma restated comparative information are not required	IAS 8.34/38
- revenue recognition rules do not differentiate between exchanges of goods of similar nature and value and exchanges of dissimilar goods, and do not discuss adjustment for the amount of cash or cash equivalents transferred in exchanges for dissimilar goods	IAS 18.12; IAS 16.21/22
- the definition of extraordinary items is broader	IAS 8.6/12
In certain enterprises, these other issues could lead to differences from IAS:	
- some parent companies do not prepare consolidated financial statements	IAS 27.7/11
- in the definition of control, it is not required that the ability to govern decision-making be accompanied by the objective of obtaining benefits from the entity's activities	IAS 27.6
- certain subsidiaries may be excluded from consolidation beyond those referred to in IAS	IAS 27.13

- a subsidiary that is a bank may be excluded from consolidation if it is dissimilar from the rest of the group	IAS 27.14
- certain set-up costs that have been paid by a company's founder can be capitalized	IAS 38.57
- internally generated brands and similar items can be capitalized if the enterprise has an exclusive legal right	IAS 38.51
- inventories are generally carried at cost rather than at the lower of cost and net realizable value; this is often not an important difference because of inflation	IAS 2.6
- the realizable value of inventories can be measured without deduction of selling costs	IAS 2.6
- certain overheads in addition to those related to production can be capitalized	IAS 2.7

Source: PricewaterhouseCoopers: Doing Business in the Russian Federation (2003)

These studies list the differences between RAS and IAS. The problem with these lists, which is not revealed in any of these publications but was discovered during the course of the interviews, is that these compiled lists of differences do not include mention of any RAS that is an abbreviated, simplified version of the English language IAS. For example, if the English version of IAS 99 is 80 pages long and the RAS on that topic is 10 pages long, IAS 99 is not included in the list of differences, even though the Russian standard is clearly not identical to the international standard. Thus, these comparative lists are deceptive because they do not reflect the true and total differences between RAS and IAS. The list is relatively short, and many items on the list are for items that are inconsequential, leading an unsophisticated reader to believe that the differences between RAS and IAS are small, when in fact the differences can be quite large for certain standards. It was pointed out during the interviews that there are really no detailed comparisons between IAS and RAS but only the superficial kind of comparisons like the one above.

Another problem with making comparisons between RAS and IAS or U.S. GAAP is historical. IAS has a historical base. International standards are based on more than 100 years of Anglo accounting evolution. Because of that, much is understood but not stated. The Russian accounting system has no such long history. So making such lists and comparisons is dangerous, in the sense that it can be misleading.

There are differences of interpretation and emphasis even within the Western market economies that have adopted IFRS or some similar set of rules. For example, a German accountant and a British accountant could interpret the same rule differently for cultural reasons. Germans are more conservative and would tend to make provisions that British accountants might not make. Germans provide for everything; British and Russian accountants provide for fewer things.

Some of the individuals interviewed stressed the point that RAS will never be identical to the international standards. They will never be a mere translation, even if every word in every international standard is translated directly into Russian. That is because Russian culture and Russian thought processes come into play. The way Russian accountants interpret the rules will always be different than the way an English accountant will interpret the language contained in the various international standards. One Russian accounting executive who worked for a Big-Four accounting firm emphasized that the problem is with interpretation, not with the translation itself, although the translation creates some complicated problems such as terminology, etc.

One reason for the differing interpretations is because of conflicts in definitions. IAS contains definitions for a great many terms. So does the Russian Civil Code. But the Civil Code definitions are often different from the IAS definitions. What is a Russian accountant to do when confronted with these differences? These differences have caused arguments with clients in the past. These definitional problems will not go away in the near future if for no other reason than because the Russian Duma (Parliament) has more important things to do than expend a lot of effort harmonizing accounting definitions with the already existing Civil Code definitions. This problem would be nonexistent if the accounting rules were formulated in the private sector, but they are not. When this possibility was mentioned to one of the partners of a Big-Four accounting firm in Russia, his reply was that he did not believe that having the private sector harmonize definitions would be better than having the Duma do it. Then, rather cynically, he added that the Duma is very much an extension of the private sector.

Another reason why RAS will never be identical to the international standards is because there is a timing lag between the time a new international standard is issued in the UK and the time that new standard is translated into Russian and adopted as part of the Russian accounting rules. This lag could be overcome if the Russian Duma made it a rule that all new international accounting standards will automatically and immediately become part of the Russian rules. However, the Duma will never make such a rule, for reasons of national pride and sovereignty. So the lag will be permanent, even though there is a theoretical solution that would correct this lag.

The degree to which the Russian accounting community understands the international standards depends on several factors. The Russian translation of the original English version of the standards was not available until late 1998. The translation was mediocre, in some respects. Part of the problem was because there were no Russian terms to convey some of the concepts. In other cases, the Russian translators simply used the wrong word or said things in such a way as to make the sentence or phrase unintelligible. In at least one case, the translator left out the word "not," with the result that the Russian version of the standard instructed the reader to do something, when in fact the

English version of the rule said *not* to do something. These kinds of mistakes and imperfections are to be expected the first time a technical document is translated, especially in cases where no terms exist for some of the words and ideas that need to be translated.

The Russian accountants who cannot read English are limited to reading the Russian translation of the international standards. That places them at a competitive disadvantage, for the reasons mentioned above. The Russian translation is mediocre in some places and in other places is downright incorrect. The Russian speaking accountant has no way of knowing how accurate the reading of a particular sentence or paragraph might be, but must rely on what is written because there is no other alternative. Russian accountants who were educated in a university that did not teach the international standards have a problem reading the international standards in any language because the standards contain concepts that the Russian accountant was never exposed to during the years at the university. Such accountants must learn the new rules as best they can, either by self-study or by attending some lectures or seminars on the various topics.

The interviews revealed that the Big-Four accounting firms have found a way around this translation problem, which gives them another competitive advantage over the local Russian firms. The Big-Four have a tendency to hire people who speak English, and at least one of the Big-Four will not hire anyone who does not speak, read and write English. The accountants who work for these firms refer to the original English version of the international standards and do not even read the Russian version, except perhaps as a secondary reference. Thus, they avoid all of the problems that are inherent in relying on the Russian translation.

Another advantage that the Big-Four firms have over their Russian-only brethren is the materials on international standards their various affiliate firms have developed over the years. The Big-Four branches in the United States, the UK and elsewhere have, over the years, developed a great deal of reading materials and some case studies that address many of the questions and problems that pop up when accountants try to apply the international standards. These materials are available to the employees of the accounting firm and also to their clients. The Big-Four firms also have regularly scheduled educational programs for their employees and clients, whereas the other Russian firms may or may not have such programs.

This wealth of educational material gives the Big-Four accounting firms an additional advantage over their Russian competitors. They can offer their clients an education that most Russian accounting firms cannot compete with. Much of the client training they provide is free. The training that they do charge for is offered at a very reasonable price. One reason for the low price is because many Russian enterprises cannot afford to pay New York or London prices. Another reason has to do with Russian culture. Russians are accustomed to getting free education. They do not see the need to pay high prices for education. This attitude affects the ability of the large accounting firms to charge a price that is high enough to meet their costs.

Another problem with the implementation of international standards that the interviews revealed is that the Russian accounting community operates as a two-tier system. The accountants who work in Moscow, St. Petersburg and a few of the other large cities are more knowledgeable about the international standards than the accountants who do not work in the large metropolitan centers. The big city accountants have more and better access to accounting materials and courses that will help them to keep current with recent developments, or even to become familiar with the basics of IAS. Accountants in the outlying regions do not have this kind of resource at their disposal. Perhaps they have internet access, which would enable them to tap into some pertinent information that is available on the net, but even internet access is not as good outside of the big cities as it is within them and it is expensive by Russian standards. However, much of the information available on the internet is useless if the accountant cannot read English, since there is much information available in English that is not available in Russian. Also, the Big-Four accounting firms do not have offices in the smaller Russian cities, so the infrastructure they carried with them to Moscow and St. Petersburg is almost totally absent outside of those two cities.

Another reason why the accountants in the outlying regions are not as knowledgeable about international standards as are the big city accountants is due to differences in demand. Most clients that need statements prepared according to international standards are in Moscow or St. Petersburg. A few big enterprises are scattered around other parts of Russia, mostly in the bigger cities. The accountants who service smaller clients have little or no need to know the international standards, so they do not take the time to learn them. The result is a two-tier system where the accountants and the employees who work for their clients in Moscow or St. Petersburg know at least something about international standards, whereas their counterparts in the outlying regions know less, or perhaps nothing about international standards.

This situation is unlikely to change soon. Some accountants, and even university professors who live in the regions have never seen the Russian translation of IAS and have not seen any Russian accounting books that discuss IAS.

The drive to adopt and implement international standards is coming more from the market than from the Russian government. Although the government is pushing for adoption and implementation of international standards, the force that is really motivating Russian enterprises to use international standards is the carrot of foreign capital. Foreign investors simply refuse to consider making loans or investing in a Russian company that does not prepare its financial statements using either IFRS or GAAP.

Russian enterprises are also under pressure from the international investing community to have their statements audited by a large foreign audit firm such as one of the Big-Four. So the process of adopting and implementing international standards is more of a bottom-up system than a top-down system. The market is causing the changes to be made where they need to be made and it is doing it faster and better than what could be accomplished by mere government decrees.

Another interesting facet of Russian accounting that the interviews revealed was how Russian accounting firms and enterprises are dealing with the new disclosure requirements. IFRS and GAAP both require much more disclosure than what Russians are accustomed to providing. Many Russian executives and accountants feel uncomfortable providing so much disclosure. Russian culture, even before the communist era, produced a closed mouth society, at least as far as revealing information to bureaucrats, government officials and the general public was concerned (Figes 2002).

Disclosure is new to the Russians and some of them do not know how to deal with it. Financial statement disclosure is sometimes more detailed than in the West, but the quality is often lower. Russian accountants tend to disclose information that has little or no value. They sometimes report extraneous information because they do not understand what is relevant for disclosure purposes. They do not always know what information is important to potential foreign investors, so they report what they are most familiar with. They provide financial statement ratios, disclose the number of employees, and so forth but sometimes leave out information that foreign investors might want to know. Some Russian financial statements are flooded with information that is of little or no use for investment decision making purposes.

Corporate Governance in Russia

As Russian firms became privatized, they went to foreign capital markets in search of investment capital. Their initial attempts at raising investment capital were extremely difficult, for a variety of reasons, some of which had to do with the accounting methods they used (Preobragenskaya and McGee 2003a). In the early stages of transition, the vast majority of Russian firms used Russian accounting standards to prepare their financial statements. That made sense when Russia was using the centralized, socialist accounting model, but western investors were not familiar with RAS and did not trust them. The main function of RAS was to provide information to the government under the old centralized system and to tax authorities under the new market system. But foreign investors require a much different focus. They are more interested in profits, disclosure and transparency. RAS did not provide sufficient information in a format that foreign investors needed, which made it very difficult for Russian firms to obtain the foreign capital they needed.

The Russian firms that wanted to raise foreign capital started issuing two sets of financial statements, one based on RAS and the other based either on IFRS or on U.S. GAAP, depending on which capital market they targeted. This dual set of financial statements presented several problems. For one, the cost of preparing two sets of financial statements greatly increased the cost of preparing financial statements. Firms could not issue just IFRS or GAAP based statements because the law and the tax authorities required RAS based statements.

Another problem they encountered was increased confusion on the part of financial statement readers. Potential investors and creditors were confronted with two different sets of financial data. Which set could they rely on? Profits, assets and a number of other items differed between the RAS based statements and the IFRS or GAAP based statements. Financial statement readers in the United States faced a similar dilemma when FASB 33 was issued in the late 1970s. That Statement required some firms to provide a full set of regular financial statements as well as supplementary statements using two different kinds of inflation accounting. The result was three different valuations for assets, which led to confusion within the accounting community.

Auditing such financial statements was another obstacle to obtaining the needed capital. Practically none of the Russian audit firms knew or used International Standards on Auditing (ISA) when they performed their audits (Preobragenskaya and McGee 2003b). The only audit firms able to perform such audits were foreign firms, mostly the Big-Five (now four) accounting firms and a few second-tier firms that were able to gain a foothold in the Russian market. This lack of ISA audits is complicated by the fact that many chief corporate accountants want an audit to be a tax audit, which is what many (but not all) audits of local companies really are.

There is also a problem of transparency, or the lack of it. A survey conducted by PricewaterhouseCoopers of transparency in 35 countries ranked Russia number 34, just ahead of China (Haigh 2001). With such a lack of transparency it is little wonder why Russian firms find it so difficult to raise foreign capital. Russia is attempting to overcome this problem by instituting good corporate governance principles such as the appointment of independent directors, establishing audit committees and insisting on more financial disclosure. However, it should be pointed out that transparency is not the only thing that drives foreign direct investment (FDI). If that were the case, Russia would be receiving more FDI than China, which is clearly not the case. Transparency is an important factor in attracting FDI, but other factors also need to be considered.

A number of detailed publications on corporate governance in Russia have been issued in recent years. One of the most frequently referred to publications is the OECD *White Paper on Corporate Governance in Russia* (2002). This publication provides detailed guidance on a number of corporate governance topics, including shareholder rights, the role of stakeholders in corporate governance, disclosure and transparency, the responsibilities of the board, and implementation and enforcement. The appendices also contain useful information on the relevant organizations and corporate governance initiatives in Russia between 1999 and 2001 and the Russian regulatory acts on corporate governance.

Upgrading Accounting Education

Part of the problem with accounting education in Russia is the perception by some bureaucrats, practitioners and educators that there is no need to upgrade accounting education. That is a stumbling block to change, since the first step in implementing any change is the recognition that change is needed. Some members of the accounting establishment in Russia have not yet reached this initial stage. The speed with which accounting education is upgraded is slowed as a result. However, the number of individuals who hold this view is decreasing with each passing year.

The people who called themselves accountants under the old Soviet system were actually bookkeepers, since practically all they did was make journal entries. In fact, there was no Russian word for accountant. They borrowed the German word for bookkeeper. Accountants were held in low esteem before 1990. Accounting was not a prestigious profession. Enthoven et al (1998) report that secondary school graduates ranked accounting 91st out of 92 occupations in terms of desirability. Changes started occurring in accounting education in 1989, but very few people were able to teach the new accounting. That is still the case, according to some of the individuals interviewed.

Another problem with upgrading accounting education is the lack of high quality educational materials. When Russia first started converting from a centralized reporting system based on a socialist model to a more decentralized market model, practically no educational materials on international standards or GAAP existed in the Russian language. The main reason for such lack of materials was because there was no need. All firms were state owned and all accounting rules and regulations were issued directly from Moscow. Even as this paper is being written not much IFRS or GAAP educational materials are available to university students in Russia.

The demand for market model accounting educational materials increased rapidly as the Russian government decided to switch to a market economic model. As state owned firms began to be privatized, they started adopting market oriented accounting models. The big firms were the first to make the changes, as they needed financial statements based either on IFRS or GAAP in order to convince foreign investors to invest in their companies.

Russian universities sometimes offered accounting courses, but when they did, it was as part of the economics faculty. There were no departments specifically devoted just to accounting at many universities, although some universities did offer accounting within a special accounting department. That is changing. Universities that never offered accounting before are now offering whole accounting programs. Some universities offer four-year programs and others offer five-year programs. Universities are trying to meet the demand for accounting by offering more courses. One constraint on offering courses to meet the demand is the difficulty of finding people to teach the courses. This problem is being solved by hiring practitioners to teach some of the courses. The Institute of Professional Accountants also runs courses to train professors in the new rules, which helps to upgrade the skills of existing professors and also increase the pool of qualified accounting professors.

Another problem Russian universities face is inertia. Most of the top professors who teach accounting are experts in the old Soviet accounting system. They have accumulated a vast knowledge of the old system and have long ago memorized the Soviet chart of accounts that all enterprises had to use to keep their books. But they need to teach the new accounting and many of them have not had any experience actually working as accountants in the new system.

Moscow State University, perhaps the best university in Russia, has very few accounting professors who are under 45 years old. The head of the accounting department is in his 70s. Perhaps these professors know the new accounting rules and methods, but if they do, it is because they learned by reading on their own and by consulting. They cannot merely parrot what they learned when they attended the university 20 or 50 years ago because the material they need to teach students today was not taught when they were students.

The interviews brought out some other interesting tid bits about university accounting education. While the professors and university administrators that were interviewed thought that the professors at their universities and in Russia in general were well qualified and up to date on the new accounting rules, the practitioners who took their courses felt differently. They felt that professors were not sufficiently trained in IFRS and that there were not enough professors to teach accounting in the universities.

The interviews also revealed that not all universities are restructuring their accounting course offerings at the same rate of speed. The universities that do the best job of teaching the new accounting are the entrepreneurial universities. There are some universities in Russia that make every effort to offer the courses demanded by the market, even though they are government institutions. As government financial support for university education is cut back, some universities are bridging the financial gap by offering a range of accounting courses and charging for them. These are the universities that offer the best programs, while other, more traditional universities are content to implement changes to their curriculum at a much slower speed.

Some of the professors who were interviewed revealed that university accounting courses are still based on RAS rather than international standards. Courses offered on the international standards explain only general concepts. One professor made the suggestion that the international standards should become the base for the entire accounting curriculum.

The course materials that Russian university students have leave something to be desired. According to one professor, there are only two books available on IAS in Russian, and neither of them is of high quality. Many Western textbooks have been translated into Russian, but some of the translations are not good and most of the books are at least one, and perhaps as many as three editions behind their English language counterparts. For example, the Russian language text may be the fourth edition, with a 1994 copyright date, whereas the same book is now available in the seventh edition in English with a 2003 copyright date.

Another problem Russian students face is the ability to get their hands on actual textbooks. Many Russian students cannot afford to buy their own copy, so they must use library copies. In some cases, this problem is alleviated by subsidizing the cost of printing the texts, but occasional subsidies are not sufficient to place books in the hands of every Russian accounting student. One of the accounting professors interviewed pointed out that the professors give students a sufficient number of handouts during class to make up for the lack of textbooks, and that these handouts are the main source of materials for exams. So perhaps the lack of textbooks is not such a big problem, assuming that the materials the professors distribute in class are of the same or higher quality than the textbooks.

The quality of accounting education is higher in Moscow and St. Petersburg than in other Russian cities for several reasons. For one, most professors outside of these two cities do not have much opportunity to practice. They just read books. Having practical experience is considered to enhance their classroom skills.

Another reason for the higher quality of education in Moscow and St. Petersburg is because the universities in the regions cannot afford to subsidize the textbook purchases of their students and their libraries cannot afford to buy a sufficient number of texts. Also, the demand for accounting professionals is less outside of the two big Russian cities, so fewer resources are used to train accounting experts. The attitude toward the accounting profession is also different in the regions. The demand for high quality is mostly in the big cities. Where the demand for high quality is low, the quality of service provided will also likely be low.

Accounting education in Russia is also being provided by several different private groups. The large international accounting firms give regular training to their staffs and also give training and seminars to their clients. Russian accounting firms also provide training to their staffs, and sometimes to their clients, but the interviews revealed that that quality of the education the smaller Russian firms provide is not at the same quality level as that provided by the big international firms.

One reason for the qualitative difference is because the large international firms have more resources to draw on than do the smaller Russian firms. The large international firms have been training their staffs and clients in international standards, modern auditing techniques and procedures for a much longer time and their various offices all over the world have developed and fine tuned their educational materials. A firm in New York or Sydney might very well develop a course or manual that can be adapted for use in Russia. The large firms have a large pool of case studies to choose from, whereas the smaller Russian accounting firms have to develop their case studies and other materials from scratch.

Another advantage the large international firms have over the smaller Russian accounting firms is that the large firms are not limited to using Russian language course materials. In fact, most of the materials they use are in English. They can use such materials because their employees know how to read English. Materials that are used to educate their non-English speaking clients can be translated into Russian as demand warrants. The Russian firms, on the other hand, are more or less limited to using available Russian language materials. The quality of these materials may be lower than what is available in English. As was previously mentioned, the 1998 Russian translation of IAS is not at the same standard as the English language original, and the Russian accounting firms tend to use the Russian version, or educational materials that are spun off of the Russian version, in their seminars and classes.

The amount and variety of the accounting training the large international accounting firms provide to their employees and clients is also larger than what most Russian firms provide. One of the Big-Four firms interviewed provides at least 40 hours a year of training for their employees, and in many cases much more than that. It gives five days of training per year just on international standards and another 6 to 12 days on various technical accounting topics, which might include international standards. It also publishes a newsletter, which is available for both employees and clients, which contains articles on recent developments. All of their employees are also involved in some kind of international certification training.

An interview with a Russian accountant who works for one of the Big-Four accounting firms revealed that the quality of international standards education in the smaller firms is of a distinctly lower quality. Each firm makes its own course materials. In smaller firms, it is often the interpretation of the instructor that is taught rather than international standards. The instructor's interpretation may be much different than reality. Most instructors do not have access to real IAS materials. They must rely on translations, many of which leave something to be desired. One Russian firm teaches a course on the IAS Chart of Accounts, which is really amusing to those who are knowledgeable about IAS, since IAS has no chart of accounts.

This problem will be solved with time, as more English speaking Russian professors write their own texts and course materials. There is a joint Tacis PricewaterhouseCoopers project that is developing course materials in the Russian language, too, so that will also help to alleviate the problem of inadequate course materials.

One question that was asked of both the large international accounting firms and the smaller Russian firms was whether the new university graduates they hired were adequately prepared. The response generally was that they were adequately prepared for entry level positions. Interestingly enough, many American accounting firms, both large and small, think that recent graduates are not adequately prepared, even though the accounting education provided by universities in America is perceived as being better than that given by universities in Russia and other Eastern European countries. Some commentators have even referred to the situation in the United States as being in crisis (Gabbin 2002; Albrecht and Sack 2000).

Perhaps one reason for the difference in perception is because the educational system in Russia and other East European countries is more rigorous than the system in the United States. Russians get more math, starting in elementary school. By the time they reach the university, their level of knowledge in math may be better than that of a junior college graduate of an American two-year college.

Another possible reason for the view that recent Russian accounting graduates are adequately prepared for entry level positions is because of the training they receive in Russian universities. The top Russian professors earn about 7,000 rubles a month ($230), so they all have to do other things to make ends meet. Many of them engage in consulting. Others work as accountants, either for a firm or on their own. This outside work exposes them to the real world of accounting and provides them with a wealth of information that is not available in textbooks. Much of what they learn in the outside world is disseminated to their students in their lectures and case studies.

Accounting Certification

Russian certification has a credibility problem because of the perception that it is not of the same standard as international certification. This perception is being reinforced by the proliferation of private accounting clubs that "travel to cities and villages selling certificates."

Russians who take the official Russian government certification exam have a higher pass rate. Pass rates on foreign exams like the American Certified Public Accountant (CPA) or Certificate in Management Accounting (CMA) or the British Association of Chartered Certified Accountants (ACCA) exams are much lower. The Russian certification exams are perceived as being more like a university exam than a western certification exam.

These foreign exams are not recognized by the Russian government, but they are recognized and highly regarded in the marketplace. Almost all of the noncertified accountants who work at the Big-Four accounting firms in Moscow and St. Petersburg are studying for one or more of these foreign certification exams, even though the exams are given only in English. This English-only option precludes a large number of Russian accountants from taking these foreign certification exams. However, it also insures that high quality will be maintained, since these exams are proctored by the sponsoring organizations or their representatives.

As the interviews were being conducted, there was a rumor that the ACCA, the largest provider of international accounting certification exams, was going to start offering at least some of the exams in Russian. Several Russian speaking countries have been pressuring the ACCA to offer the exam in Russian for a number of years. Latin American countries have been pressuring the ACCA to offer its exams in Spanish as well. That is because ACCA certification is recognized in more than 160 countries, which gives its certificate holders immediate international recognition. ACCA has been hesitant to offer its exams in languages other than English for a variety of reasons, including cost and security. Offering the ACCA exams in Russian, or in other languages, would go a long way toward spreading knowledge about IFRS, since the ACCA exams test on IFRS. Several months after the interviews were concluded, the ACCA announced that it would offer some exams in the Russian language.

One private organization has started a 400 hours program to make certified accountants. A few centers prepare people for the certification exams in Moscow, St. Petersburg and the Urals. Accountants in other locations have to learn either from their employers or on their own. Hock Accountancy Training is perhaps the largest private provider of accounting certification training in Russia. It has training facilities in several cities and also has distance education programs available to help accountants pass the American

CPA, CMA and CFM exams. Hock also does IFRS training to a lesser extent. A number of private firms offer ACCA training.

There will be a demand for foreign certification exams in Russia as long as there is no credible Russian qualification. Russian certification is in statutory accounting. There is a movement to adopt an international certification model but it will be some time before such a movement has a finished product to offer to the Russian accounting community. Until Russia restructures its certification and shifts toward something that resembles international certification, the demand for foreign certification will remain strong.

Both of the Russian audit firms that participated in the interviews indicated a desire to establish a relationship with accountants who had foreign certification so that they could better serve their clients and so that they could expand their business into new markets. Perhaps the best way for Russia to approach certification would be to fully recognize truly international certification such as the CPA or ACCA and merely require those who want to be certified in Russia to pass exams on Russian business law and taxation. A similar method is being used in the EU and seems to be working well.

There is a movement to obtain outside assistance to establish an internationally recognized certification. Tacis and USAID have attempted to establish a regional certification in Central Asia and they want to open an office in Russia. The Central Asian model is based on CIMA, so it is likely that the Russian model will at least take a look at the CIMA model.

CONCLUDING COMMENTS

As a partner in one of the large international accounting firms stated, the three most important factors that international investors consider are who their partner is, whether the financial statements are transparent and whether the statements were prepared using either international standards or GAAP. Foreign investors are not at all interested in reading statements prepared using RAS, not only because they are not well versed in RAS, but also because they do not believe that the Russian statutory accounting rules provide good accounting information. Accounting reform is an essential ingredient of economic independence (Ichizli & Zacchea 2000)

Then there is the problem of what is called black cash. Not all transactions are recorded. The Russians have devised ingenious ways to evade taxes. Applying the international standards or GAAP to a company's books will not solve this problem if some important transactions are never included in the books. President Putin has instituted a low flat corporate (24%) and individual (13%) income tax, which will take away some of the incentive for playing tax evasion games, but tax rates that are low by European standards will not totally end the practice, since tax evasion is seen as not only a way to reduce taxes but also as a game.

Another question is how long it will take the rest of Russia to catch up to Moscow and St. Petersburg, in terms of the level of sophistication of financial reporting and in terms of accounting education. The only thing that can be said for sure is that it will take a long time. The process is market driven. Specific enterprises and regions will catch up as the market demands quality financial information. The speed with which the various regions will approach the Moscow – St. Petersburg standard will depend on whether international investors have an interest in investing in a particular enterprise or region, and on whether that enterprise is interested enough in attracting foreign capital to prepare its financial statements using some internationally accepted standard like IFRS or GAAP.

Another structural problem that needs to be overcome is the lack of knowledge of international standards on the part of the clients that retain the services of the large accounting firms. One partner who was interviewed revealed that only two of the accountants at one of the top Russian enterprises had any knowledge of the international standards whatsoever. This low level of knowledge makes it more difficult for any accounting firm to provide the proper services. Over time, this problem will shrink in importance, as the accounting firms train their clients and as a new crop of accounting graduates take their places in the accounting departments of these enterprises. But this process takes time.

There was some disagreement as to whether the level of accounting education would improve faster in accounting firms or in universities. The professors who were interviewed in St. Petersburg and Moscow thought that accounting education would improve faster in the universities. The reason they gave is that their professors are also engaged as outside consultants and they bring their knowledge into the classrooms.

But practitioners responded differently to this question. Especially in the case of the large international firms, there was the perception that the materials they provided for instruction and the resources they had to draw upon were of superior quality to those available in universities. Also, it could be mentioned again that the materials the international firms use for their training are often in English, whereas university materials are in Russian, so the universities have a translation problem to deal with that the big firms do not have to face. When this point was raised in the course of the interviews with university professors, they replied that this inherent weakness could be overcome by the professors, who would correct any mistakes in the course materials. But while this may be true in some cases, it probably is not true in all cases, especially in those cases where the professor is not able to read the international standards in the original English. In such cases, the professors will have to rely on the Russian translation, and they are likely to repeat the mistakes that are contained in the translated materials.

It will take a long time to fully implement international standards in Russia. The process is ongoing. However, it will happen, at least to some extent. If government continues to dominate the rulemaking process, RAS will never be identical to the international standards, for the several reasons mentioned above. But if the market takes over, Russian enterprises that want to attract foreign capital will prepare their financial statement using the international standards anyway. Government involvement in the standard setting process will merely serve to complicate accounting and make it more expensive.

REFERENCES

Albrecht, W. Steve & Robert J. Sack. 2002. *Accounting Education: Charting the Course through a Perilous Future.* Sarasota, FL: American Accounting Association [www.aaahq.org/pubs/AESv16/toc.htm].
An EYe on Russia, monthly newsletter published by the Ernst & Young Russia office [www.ey.com/global/content.nsf/Russia_E/Home].
Bailey, Derek T. 1982. Accounting in Russia: The European Connection. *International Journal of Accounting* 18(1), 1-36.
Campbell, Robert W. 1963. *Accounting in Soviet Planning and Management.* Russian Research Center Series 45, Cambridge, Harvard University Press.
Campbell, Robert W. 1956. Accounting for Depreciation in the Soviet Economy. *Quarterly Journal of Economics* 70(4), 481-506.
Chastain, C.E. 1982. Soviet Accounting Lags Behind the Needs of Enterprise Managers. *Management International Review* 22(4), 12-18.
The Code of Professional Conduct of Independent Directors. 2003. Independent Director (newsletter), Spring, p. 11. [www.nand.ru]
Collingwood, H. 1991. The Soviets Take Accounting 101. *Business Week,* April 22, p.38.
Corporate Governance Code, Russian Institute of Directors http://www.rid.ru/db.php?db_id=516&l=en
Enthoven, Adolf J.H., Yaroslav V. Sokolov, Svetlana M. Bychkova, Valery V. Kovalev & Maria V. Semenova. 1998. *Accounting, Auditing and Taxation in the Russian Federation.* Montvale, NJ: Institute of Management Accountants & The Center for International Accounting Development, The University of Texas at Dallas.
Enthoven, Adolf J.H., Jaroslav V. Sokolov and Alexander M. Petrachkov. 1992. *Doing Business in Russia and the Other Former Soviet Republics:*

Accounting and Joint Venture Issues. Montvale, NJ: Institute of Management Accountants.

Ermakova, Tatiana. 2003. Tax Authorities Clarify Issues Regarding the Application of Chapter 25 of the Tax Code. *Legislative News*, July, pp. 1-5 [www.deloitte.ru].

Figes, Orlando. 2002. *Natasha's Dance: A Cultural History of Russia*. New York: Henry Holt and Company.

Friedman, Milton & Rose D. Friedman. 1984. *Tyranny of the Status Quo*. New York: Harcourt Brace Jovanovich.

GAAP Convergence 2002: A Survey of National Efforts to Promote and Achieve Convergence with International Financial Reporting Standards. 2002. BDO, Deloitte Touche Tohmatsu, Ernst & Young, Grant Thornton, KPMG & PricewaterhouseCoopers. Researched by Donna L. Street. [www.pwcglobal.com]

GAAP 2001: A Survey of National Accounting Rules Benchmarked against International Accounting Standards. 2001. A joint publication of Andersen, BDO, Deloitte Touche Tohmatsu, Ernst & Young, Grant Thornton, KPMG and PricewaterhouseCoopers, edited by Christopher W. Nobes. [www.kpmg.ru] [www.ifad.net]

GAAP 2000: A Survey of National Accounting Rules in 53 Countries. 2000. A joint publication of Arthur Andersen, BDO, Deloitte Touche Tohmatsu, Ernst & Young International, Grant Thornton, KPMG and PricewaterhouseCoopers, edited by Christopher W. Nobes. [www.pwcglobal.com]

Gabbin, Alexander L. 2002. The Crisis in Accounting Education. *Journal of Accountancy*, April, pp. 81-86.

Garrod, Neil & Stuart McLeay (Eds.). 1996. *Accounting in Transition: The Implications of Political and Economic Reform in Central Europe.* London & New York: Routledge.

Gorelik, George. 1974a. Notes on the Development and Problems of Soviet Uniform Accounting. *International Journal of Accounting* 9(2), 135-148.

Gorelik, George. 1974b. Soviet Accounting, Planning and Control. *Abacus* 10(1), 13-25.

Gorelik, George. 1971. Enterprise Profit and Profitability Measurements: Soviet-American Convergence. *International Journal of Accounting* 6(2), 1-14.

Haigh, Art. 2001. We View Russia's Future with Optimism. *Kommersant-Daily*, January 26 [www.pwcglobal.ru/].

Hayek, Friedrich A. (ed.) 1935. *Collectivist Economic Planning: Critical Studies on the Possibilities of Socialism,* London: George Routledge & Sons, Ltd., reprinted by Augustus M. Kelley Publishers, Clifton, NJ, 1975.

Hoff, Trygve J.B. 1981. *Economic Calculation in the Socialist Society.* Indianapolis: Liberty Press.

Horwitz, Bertrand. 1970. Accounting Controls and the Soviet Economic Reforms. *California Management Review* 13(1), 75-83.

Horwitz, Bertrand. 1963. Depreciation and Cost Stability in Soviet Accounting. *Accounting Review* 38(4), 819-826.

ICAR Newsletter [www.icar.ru/] various issues.

Ichizli, Svetlana M. & Nicholas M. Zacchea. 2000. Accounting Reform in the Former Soviet Republics: An Essential Ingredient for Economic Independence. *Government Accountants Journal* 49(2), 46-53.

The Independent Directors Association Charter. 2003. *Independent Director,* Spring, p.12. [www.nand.ru].

Jaruga, Alicja. 1996. Accounting in Socialist Countries: The Beginnings of Reform. In Neil Garrod & Stuart McLeay (eds.), *Accounting in Transition: The Implications of Political and Economic Reform in Central Europe* (pp. 12-27). London & New York: Routledge.

Kobrack, F. & G. Feldman. 1991. Is There an Accounting Textbook Market in the Soviet Union? *Publishers Weekly,* September 20, pp. 43-44.

KPMG 2003. *Doing Business in Russia.* July [www.kpmg.ru].

KPMG. *Russia – Tax Overview* [www.kpmg.ru].

Lange, Oskar. 1937. On the Economic Theory of Socialism, II, *Review of Economic Studies* 4(2), 123-42.

Lange, Oskar. 1936. On the Economic Theory of Socialism, I. *Review of Economic Studies* 4(1), 53-71.

Lebow, Marc I. & Rasoul H. Tondkar. 1986. Accounting in the Soviet Union. *International Journal of Accounting* 22(1), 61-79.

Legislative Tracking, Deloitte & Touche newsletter [www.deloitte.ru].

Lerner, Abba P. 1935. Economic Theory and Socialist Economy. *Review of Economic Studies* 2, 51-61.

Lippincott, Benjamin E. (Ed.). 1938. *On the Economic Theory of Socialism.* Minneapolis: University of Minnesota Press.

McGee, Robert W. 2003a. Educating Professors in a Transition Economy: A Case Study of Bosnia & Herzegovina. Proceedings of the Twelfth World Business Congress, International Management Development Association, Vancouver, BC, Canada, June 25-29, 2003, pp. 155-162. Available at [www.ssrn.com].

McGee, Robert W. 2003b. Reforming Accounting Education in a Transition Economy: A Case Study of Armenia. Proceedings of the Twelfth World Business Congress, International Management Development Association, Vancouver, BC, Canada, June 25-29, 2003, pp. 139-146. Available at [www.ssrn.com].

Mills, Robert H. & Abbott L. Brown. 1966. Soviet Economic Development and Accounting. *Journal of Accountancy* 121(6), 40-46.

Mises, Ludwig von. 1935. Economic Calculation in the Socialist Commonwealth. In Friedrich A. Hayek (Ed.), *Collectivist Economic Planning: Critical Studies on the Possibilities of Socialism* (pp. 87-130) London: George Routledge & Sons, Ltd., reprinted by Augustus M. Kelley Publishers, Clifton, NJ, 1975.

Mises, Ludwig von. 1923. Neue Beitrage zum Problem der sozialistischen Wirtschaftsrechnung [New Contributions to the Problem of Socialist Economic Calculation], *Archiv fur Sozialwissenschaft und Sozial Politik* 51, December, pp. 488-500.

Mises, Ludwig von. 1922. *Die Gemeinwirtschaft.* The second German edition (1932) was translated into English by J. Kahane and published as *Socialism: An Economic and Sociological Analysis* by Jonathan Cape, London, 1936.

Mises, Ludwig von. 1920. Die Wirtschaftsrechnung im Sozialistischen Gemeinwesen [Economic Calculation in the Socialist Commonwealth]. *Archiv fur Sozialwissenschaft und Sozialpolitik* 47, 86-121.

Motyka, Wolodymyr. 1990. The Impact of Western Europe on Accounting Development in Tsarist Russia Prior to 1800. *Abacus* 26(1), 36-62.

OECD. 2002. *White Paper on Corporate Governance in Russia.* April 23. Paris: OECD. www.oecd.org/dataoecd/10/3/2789982.pdf.

Polanyi, Karl. 1923. Sozialistiche Rechnungslegung [Socialistic Accounting], *Archiv fur Sozialwissenschaft und Sozialpolitik* 49, 377-420.

Preobragenskaya, Galina G. & Robert W. McGee. 2003a. International Accounting Standards and Foreign Direct Investment in Russia. Presented at the International Trade and Finance Association's Thirteenth International Conference, Vaasa, Finland, May 28-31, 2003. [www.ssrn.com]

Preobragenskaya, Galina G. & Robert W. McGee. 2003b. The Current State of Auditing in Russia. In Jerry Biberman & Abbass F. Alkhafaji (Eds.), *Business Research Yearbook: Global Business Perspectives*, Volume X (pp.499-503) Saline, MI: McNaughton & Gunn, Inc. A longer version of this paper is posted at [www.ssrn.com].

PricewaterhouseCoopers. 2003. *Doing Business in the Russian Federation.* [www.pwcglobal.com/ru].

Richard, Jacques. 1998. Accounting in Eastern Europe: From Communism to Capitalism. In Peter Walton, Axel Haller & Bernard Raffournier (Eds.), *International Accounting* (pp. 295-323). London: International Thomson Business Press.

Rothbard, Murray N. 1991. The End of Socialism and the Calculation Debate Revisited. *Review of Austrian Economics* 5(2), 51-76.

Rozhnova, Olga. 2000. The Problem of Perception of the New Russian Accounting Standards. *ICAR Newsletter*, November/December.

Russia – Legislative News, Deloitte & Touche newsletter [www.deloitte.ru].

Russian Legislation website, Ernst & Young [www.tax.eycis.com].

Schneidman, Leonid. 2003. "The Long Road to IAS." *Kommersant*, June 9 [www.pwcglobal.com/ru].

Scott, George M. 1969. Accounting and Economic Reform in the Soviet Union. *Abacus* 5(1), 55-63.

Sennholz, Hans. 2002. Russia's March from Communism. September 12, Auburn, AL: Mises Institute. [www.mises.org].

Shama, Avraham & Christopher G. McMahan. 1990. Perestroika and Soviet Accounting: From a Planned to a Market Economy. *International Journal of Accounting* 25(3), 155-168.

Street, Donna L. 2002. GAAP 2001 – Benchmarking National Accounting Standards against IAS: Summary of Results. *Journal of International Accounting, Auditing & Taxation* 11, 77-90.

Thornton, Judith. 1983. Twenty-Five Years of Soviet National Income Accounting: From Adjusted Factor Cost to Ultra-Adjusted Factor Cost. *ACES Bulletin* 25(3), 53-67.

Transition Newsletter, World Bank Group [www.transitionnewsletter/]. Various issues.

Turk, Ivan & Neil Garrod. 1996. The Adaptation of International Accounting Rules: Lessons from Slovenia. In Neil Garrod & Stuart McLeay (Eds.), *Accounting in Transition: The Implications of Political and Economic Reform in Central Europe* (pp. 141-162) London & New York: Routledge.

Chapter 3

THE CURRENT STATE OF AUDITING IN RUSSIA*

Abstract

This paper presents an overview of the current state of auditing in Russia. International Standards on Auditing (ISA) are in the process of being adopted and implemented but this task is far from complete. Furthermore, there is resistance to ISA adoption and there is less than a widespread perception that they are needed or desirable. Russia has adopted some auditing rules that are not included in ISA and the focus of audits in many companies is tax compliance or minimization rather than attestation. Lack of full compliance with ISA makes it more difficult to attract investment capital, since foreign investors do not place much confidence in financial statements that do not comply with International Accounting Standards and that were not audited using ISA.

INTRODUCTION

Audit reform is one of the Russian government's key priorities. Russia needs an infusion of capital to replenish the erosion of the capital base that has taken place since the start of the communist regime in 1917, but capital is not readily forthcoming, for a variety of reasons. For one, there is competition for the world's capital. Russian investments have to compete with investments in more than 100 other countries and many investors see Russia as a relatively undesirable place to invest.

The *Index of Economic Freedom*, published jointly by the Wall Street Journal and the Heritage Foundation, is a key reference for international investors who are trying to decide where to invest. The most recent annual edition (2003) shows that Russia ranked 135 in terms of economic freedom, out of 156 countries whose statistics were included in the study (Table 3). Its overall score for 2003, which averages ten categories, is 3.70, on a scale from 1 to 5, where 1 is the most free. That score has remained constant since 2000

---

* An earlier version of this chapter was presented at the 15th Annual Conference of the International Academy of Business Disciplines, Orlando, Florida, USA, April 3-6, 2003.

but is somewhat worse than the scores it received in earlier years (See Table 1).

One of the relative bright spots was the score it received for foreign investment (3.0), which was the second best score of the ten categories included in the study (See Table 2). Although a score of 3.0 is not good enough to excite foreign investors, it is one of the best things the Russian economy has going for it at present. So it makes sense from a policy perspective to do things that will enhance the desire to invest in Russia. Russian President Putin's decision to adopt a low, flat tax (Klebnikov 2001) has helped to attract foreign capital as has the spread of the rule of law (Williams 2001), which calms investors' anxieties. But that is not enough to attract capital.

Financial transparency is important to foreign investors (Radoutsky 2001). The credibility of financial statements is crucial. If the financial statements cannot be trusted, it is extremely difficult to attract foreign investment because investors cannot be confident of what they are investing in. Furthermore, the evidence shows that Russian financial statements do not inspire much confidence (Rozhnova 2000; Currie 1996). One way to enhance financial statement transparency is to use some internationally recognized system of financial reporting. Russia is making moves in that direction by adopting International Accounting Standards (IAS), which are recognized in dozens of countries. But merely stating that a company uses IAS is not sufficient to win investor confidence. A reliable, trustworthy audit system must be in place to verify that the standards are actually being used. That is where the audit function comes in. An auditing system based on International Standards of Auditing (ISA) provides the much needed oversight of commercial and government activities that is needed to instill confidence in the reliability of financial information (Ichizli and Zacchea 2000).

Russia's transformation from a centrally planned economy to a market system has been difficult in a number of ways. The government decided several years ago to adopt IAS but the process is still incomplete (ICAR 1999). Some standards have been adopted while others have not (Ramcharran 2000). Furthermore, even where a standard on a particular topic has been adopted, the Russian standard is not identical to the international standard (ICAR 2000a, b).

Another problem with adopting IAS is that the Russian accountants, auditors and bookkeepers who must implement and use the new rules are not always as knowledgeable about the rules as they should be. Educating a whole nation takes time and is complicated by the fact that there is a shortage of people who are qualified to teach the new accounting (Shaw et al. 2000) and there is a shortage of good course material (Coyle and Platonov 1998; Anon. 1994). The education process has been ongoing for more than ten years but is far from complete (Cheney 1990). Although Russia adopted a new chart of accounts (Paliy 2000), the chart of accounts is the least of Russia's problems. What it needs is accountants, bookkeepers and auditors who know the rules and know how to apply them. The United States Agency for International Development (USAID) and other organizations (Anon. 2002a) have provided funding to train members of the Russian accounting profession, but the funding to date has been small and piecemeal (Anon. 2001a; Cornish 1999).

THE STATE OF AUDITING IN RUSSIA

Auditing is a relatively new profession in Russia. The first audit company (Inaudit) was founded by special decree (Postanovlenie) by the Soviet Ministry of SSSR in 1987. Since 1992 the income tax law required companies having foreign investments or foreign companies to present an independent auditor's opinion as part of their financial statements that must be submitted to the Tax Revenue Service. There are now thousands of audit firms in Russia.

Russian auditors face many of the same problems that Russian accountants and bookkeepers face. The rules have changed since many auditors left school, so they must learn the new rules. The problem is that there aren't enough qualified instructors to teach the new rules and the quality of teaching materials is not always as good as it could be. Until recently, accounting and auditing materials had to be translated from other languages, since materials like the International Accounting Standards (IAS) and International Standards on Auditing (ISA) were not available in the Russian language. Those materials, as well as several good textbooks have now been translated. But what is more important, Russian authors have started writing their own textbooks and course materials, a development that is significant, since it eliminates the translation problems that invariably occur when foreign texts have to be translated into another language.

Another problem Russian auditors face is that many companies either use only some IAS, or they use not only IAS but also Russian Accounting Standards (RAS), which are not always the same as IAS (Vysokov 2000). Russian tax rules rely on RAS, whereas financial reports are often constructed using at least some of the IAS. Furthermore, the accounting software is not always able to convert RAS to IAS and vice versa. So auditors are faced with the task of trying to verify different sets of books that utilize two different sets of accounting standards.

Russian auditors face other problems as well. For example, the Russian business culture, after three generations of communist rule, has become corrupt. There is also a lack of disclosure and transparency. Many transactions between related parties are not disclosed. Money laundering is common and widespread. Western banks and stock markets sometimes participate in the money laundering process (Burns 1999). Russian auditors somehow have to deal with these structural problems and widespread practices. Methods have to be found to deal with these problems and auditors have to be trained so that they know what to look for and what to do when they find it.

The prevalence of barter is another roadblock in the path of good audits. Barter is popular, especially since the devaluation of the Ruble in 1998. Russia's oil and gas industry resorts to barter quite frequently. The problem with the widespread use of barter is that barter can obscure financial results and weaken the implementation of IAS. Foreign investors want to have confidence in the fairness of financial statements, and having the widespread use of barter does not bolster that confidence (Lindberg 2002).

Audit procedures in Russia have tightened up in recent years. It used to be that different auditors applied different standards, and while that is still true to a certain extent, audit standards are becoming more uniform and harmonized as more Russian audit firms adopt and implement ISA (Anon. 1997). On July 29, 2002 the Council on Audit at the Russian Finance Ministry approved drafts of audit standards that are similar to ISA (Anon. 2002b). Some Russian firms have been using ISA for several years, but now that the Finance Ministry has approved international standards, they will become increasingly widespread. However, having some government issue a decree that such standards must be used does not mean that they will be used in every case. It will take some time for the new audit standards to permeate the system and the minds of Russian auditors.

The approach to audits in Russia is also different than the approach used in the West. Before the collapse of the Soviet Union there were no auditors, in the Western sense of the term (Enthoven et al. 1998). Accounting glossaries as recent as 1990 did not even include the word "auditor." The traditional Russian approach, going back to the time of the Tsars, had more to do with control and inspection than with checking and verifying in the Western sense (Bychkova 1996; Enthoven et al. 1998). That approach is now changing.

Perhaps it is not fair to compare audits in Russia to audits in Western market economies such as the United States. However, comparisons have been made. Current and former employees of Arthur Andersen, Deloitte Touche Tohmatsu, Ernst & Young, KPMG International and PricewaterhouseCoopers have cited the lack of accounting standards and oversight that exists in Russia. They have said that firms engage in auditing practices in Russia that would be considered unethical or illegal if done in the United States. Disguising company profits is one practice that was mentioned (Tavernise 2002).

Western audit firms have also come under criticism because of questionable audits. PricewaterhouseCoopers' audit of Gazprom, a Russian petroleum and natural gas company, is only the most prominent of several such audits that have come under fire (Chazan and Whalen 2002). One question that arose during the course of this audit was whether Gazprom executives were enriching themselves at the expense of their shareholders. The evidence suggests that they were. The problem, from an audit perspective, is that prior year audits by PWC failed to uncover such conduct. As a result, PWC is being sued (Anon. 2001b)

RUSSIAN AUDIT STANDARDS

Russian audit standards are similar, but not identical to International Standards on Auditing (ISA). A detailed study comparing the Russian rules to ISA found that many differences exist, some of them substantive (Bychkova and Lebedeva 2001). There are several reasons for the differences. For one, The 1999 ISA bound volume was the one that was translated into Russian, so any changes to ISA that took place after that volume was published are not automatically a part of the Russia audit rules. Second, Russia has adopted at least six audit rules that are not included in ISA (Danilevsky et al 2001). These six extra rules incorporate specific features of the Russian audit system. These rules are:

- Description of Related Services and Their Requirements,
- Requirements for Internal Standards of Audit Firms,
- Rights and Obligations of Audit Firms and Audited Entities,
- Procedures for entering into Audit Engagement Contracts,
- Written Information on Audit Results Provided by the Auditor to the Management of Economic Entity, and
- Auditor's Education.

These six Russian rules either are not covered in ISA or are imbedded in various other standards. There are good and valid reasons for these six extra rules. For example, the rule on "Rights and Obligations" was made because of the widespread perception on the part of some clients that the audit rules do not apply to them (Danilevsky et al 2001).

In a sense, it can be said that the Russian rules are more comprehensive than ISA because Russian auditors have six rules that ISA does not have. But on the other hand, Russian auditors do not have any of the rules that were added to ISA after the 1999 translation into Russian, unless the Russian government or other private group translated the post-1999 rules into Russian.

The fact that the Russian rules are not identical to ISA causes at least two problems. For one, the financial reports that companies issue cannot state that ISA were applied unless *all* International Standards on Auditing were applied. That causes a credibility problem in international capital markets because investors cannot place full confidence in financial statements where only some International Accounting Standards were applied.

Secondly, the fact that Russia does not think it is important to have rules that mirror IAS means that it is unlikely that Russia will have audit rules that are substantially identical to ISA any time soon, which means the problem will persist, thus placing Russian enterprises at a competitive disadvantage in international capital markets.

Another structural problem with the Russian auditing system is that there is a time lag between the time an ISA is adopted or amended and the time that word of the change is disseminated to the Russian audit community. In the case of the Russian translation of the 1999 ISA bound volume, for example, the translation was not completed until October 2000 (Remizov 2001), so there was a lag of about one year between the time the latest ISAs were published in English and the time they appeared in Russian. This information time lag was actually more than a year, since the Russian audit community did not instantaneously absorb the contents of the newly published Russian version. It took time to publish and distribute the Russian version and many Russian auditors did not see any pressing need to buy the book, since there was the perception on the part of many Russian auditors that they didn't need it.

This brings to mind another, related problem with the adoption and implementation of ISA. Many Russian auditors think that they are complying with ISA even though they have not actually read them and do not understand them. The same can be said of the Russian audit rules. Many Russian auditors have not read the Russian rules either, yet they are confident that they comply with them. Many Russian auditors feel that if their clients are satisfied and if there are no claims filed against them, then they have complied with the rules. Other Russian auditors think that they do not need to comply with ISA because Russia has its own audit rules (Remizov 2001).

A substantial segment of the Russian financial community still believes that ISA should not be implemented. Most Russian clients are more interested in minimizing their taxes than in abstract concepts of attestation and fair presentation of financial information. Furthermore, it is advantageous to issue untrue and unfair statements for tax purposes. Many clients do not see the need to pay fees for Western style audits, since they are perceived has having limited value and can result in actually increasing tax liability (Remizov 2001),

One solution to this dilemma would be for auditors to issue an audit opinion only if they comply with all (or most) ISAs, and refer to any other kind of audit engagement as a review or something else, but not an audit. Not all Russian companies need to attract international capital, so this suggestion would alleviate at least part of the problem, unless some government decree requires ISA audits.

Another problem with adopting and implementing ISA is that ISA audits are more complicated and expensive than traditional audits. Russian auditors who want to perform an audit in compliance with ISA are at a competitive disadvantage because of price and they often have to persuade clients that such an audit is worth the extra cost.

Some commentators have advocated the use of coercion to speed the adoption and use of ISA (Remizov 2001). However, coercion is the opposite of the market. Markets develop and prosper because of some consumer need, in the absence of some government impediment. If ISA audits are to become popular and widespread, first there must be a demand for them. In an economy that is attempting to throw off the old, centrally planned system and replace it with markets, using coercion is a step in the wrong direction.

Another question that must be raised, if coercion is decided upon as the solution to the lack of demand for ISA audits, is who will do the coercing. The two options are the government or some quasi-private group of accountants or auditors. In either case, the individuals doing the coercing probably will not be adequately versed in ISA. Russian auditors themselves are not yet fully versed in ISA, partly because the Russian translation only recently appeared and also because the Russian translation does not include all of the ISAs, but only some of them. It is also unlikely that the individuals chosen to do the coercing will be the most intelligent auditors from the available pool. Just like government bureaucrats in the West are usually not as intelligent as the individuals they are called on to regulate and coerce, it is likely that the Russian bureaucrats chosen to do the job of coercing will not be as intelligent as the individuals they will be checking.

That can lead to at least two problems. Intelligent individuals in the private sector can fool the coercive bureaucrats because they are more familiar with the rules. But also, and perhaps more importantly, the bureaucrats, because they may not have a firm grasp of the rules, may pressure firms to do things that are in violation of the rules. Thus, their attempts at coercion would be counterproductive. Not only would they be using coercion, but also they would be using it in a way that defeats the purpose of the coercion in the first place.

CONCLUDING COMMENTS

Russian auditors face a number of problems. There is a time lag between the time a new ISA is passed and the time it is translated into Russian. There is another time lag between the time the new rule is translated and the time auditors can get their hands on it, read it, understand it and start implementing it. Furthermore, there is less than total agreement on the value of ISA in the first place, so the incentive to fully and rapidly implement ISA is lacking. Many clients don't want ISA audits, both because of the perception that such audits are not worth the cost and because such audits could increase their tax liability. Many auditors do not see the value in them, either. If there is little demand and only a small supply of audit firms willing and able to do ISA audits, then few audits will get done.

Then there is the problem that Russian audit rules are not identical with ISA. Russia has some rules that are not present in ISA and ISA has some rules that have not yet been adopted in Russia. That fact does little to reassure international investors that the financial statements they are reading are credible and transparent.

In spite of all these drawbacks, barriers and structural problems, the Russian stock market performed rather well in recent years, compared to those in Western Europe and the United States. So the fact that the current state of Russian auditing leaves something to be desired does not mean that Russian enterprises will not be able to raise capital. It will just make the job more difficult and will raise the cost of capital.

Table 1
Russia's Economic Freedom Score

Year	Score
2003	3.70
2002	3.70
2001	3.70
2000	3.70
1999	3.50
1998	3.35
1997	3.55
1996	3.50
1995	3.40

Table 2
Score for Each Category
(2003)

Category	Score
Trade Policy	4.0
Government Intervention	2.5
Foreign Investment	3.0
Wages and Prices	3.0
Regulation	4.0
Fiscal Burden	3.5
Monetary Policy	5.0
Banking and Finance	4.0
Property Rights	4.0
Black Market	4.0

Table 3
Russia's Relative Ranking

Year	Russia's Rank	Countries in Survey
2003	135	156
2002	131	156
2001	127	155
2000	122	161
1999	110	161
1998	95	156
1997	106	150
1996	93	142
1995	69	101

REFERENCES

Anon. 2002a. CIMA Supports Ongoing Russian Management Accounting Reform. *Financial Management* (July/August): 46.

Anon. 2002b. Russia Heads for International Accounting Standards. *International Tax Review* 13:8 (September): 4.

Anon. 2001a. Accountants in Russia Gain International Skills. *Financial Management* (April): 44.

Anon. 2001b. Dirt Leaks Out. *Economist* July 7, p. 62.

Anon. 1997. Russian Auditors Can Now Work to Unified Standards. *Current Digest of the Post Soviet Press*. 49:27, August 6, p. 12.

Anon. 1994. Tanya Bondarenko Seeks American Education. *Baylor Business Review* 12:1 (Spring): 12-15.

Burns, Stuart. 1999. Original Sin. *Accountancy*, October, p. 42.

Bychkova, Svetlana. 1996. The Development and Status of Auditing in Russia. *The European Accounting Review* 5:1, 77-90.

Bychkova, Svetlana and Natalya Lebedeva. 2001. Comparing the Russian Auditing Regulations against Western Standards. *Accounting Report* (ICAR) (January/February): 24-28. [www.icar.ru]

Chazan, Guy and Jeanne Whalen. 2002. Russia to Probe Pricewaterhouse's Audits of Gazprom. *Wall Street Journal*, February 20, p. A16.

Cheney, Glenn Alan. 1990. Western Accounting Arrives in Eastern Europe. *Journal of Accountancy* (September): 40-43.

Cornish, Keith. 1999. Taking IASs to Russia. *Accountancy* 124: 1271 (July): 54.

Coyle, William H. and Vladimir V. Platonov. 1998. Insights Gained from International Exchange and Educational Initiatives between Universities. *Issues in Accounting Education* 13:1 (February): 223-33.

Currie, Antony. 1996. The Figures Behind the Figures. *Euromoney*, Issue 330, October, pp. 89-91.

Danilevsky, Yuri, Oleg Ostrovsky and Eugeny Guttsait. 2001. Russian Audit Standards: Past, Present and Future. *Accounting Report* (ICAR) (January/February): 1, 9-11. [www.icar.ru]

Enthoven, Adolf J.H., Yaroslav V. Sokolov, Svetlana M. Bychkova, Valery V. Kovalev and Maria V. Semenova. 1998. *Accounting, Auditing and Taxation in the Russian Federation.* Published jointly by the Foundation for Applied Research, The Institute of Management Accountants, Montvale, New Jersey and The Center for International Accounting Development, The University of Texas at Dallas, Richardson, Texas.

Index of Economic Freedom. 2003. New York: The Wall Street Journal and Washington,   DC: The   Heritage   Foundation [www.heritage.org/research/features/index/]

International Center for Accounting Reform (ICAR). 2000a. *Accounting Reform Recommendations* [www.icar.ru/eng/report.zip]

International Center for Accounting Reform (ICAR). 2000b. The Accounting Reform Recommendations. *Accounting Report* (ICAR), October 3, 2000 [www.icar.ru/eng/newsletter/3.10.2000.html]

International Center for Accounting Reform (ICAR). 1999. *Considerations concerning the establishment of accounting standards in the Russian Federation*, September.

Ichizli, Svetlana M. and Nicholas M. Zacchea. 2000. Accounting Reform in the Former Soviet Republics: An Essential Ingredient for Economic Independence. *The Government Accountants Journal* 49:2 (Summer): 46-53.

Klebnikov, Paul. 2001. A Putin Play. *Forbes* 168:8 (October 1): 128.

Lindberg, Deborah L. 2002. The Use of Barter Hampers Implementation of International Accounting Standards and Contributes to Financial Woes in the Russian Federation. *Russian & East European Finance and Trade* 38:3 (May/June): 5-17.

Paliy, Vitaly. 2000. New Chart of Accounts Approved. *Accounting Report* (ICAR), December. [www.icar.ru]

Radoutsky, Alexander. 2001. Transparent Financial Information as a Factor of Economic Stability and Intensive Growth. *Accounting Report* (ICAR) (March/April): 18-19.
[www.icar.ru/eng/newsletter/pdf/4.2001.pdf]

Ramcharran, Harri. 2000. The Need for International Accounting Harmonization: An Examination and Comparison of the Practices of Russian Banks. *American Business Review* 18:1 (January) 1-8.

Remizov, Nikolai. 2001. Issues of ISA Implementation in Russia. *Accounting Report* (ICAR) (January/February): 22-24. [www.icar.ru]

Rozhnova, Olga. 2000. The Problem of Perception of New Russian Accounting Standards. *Accounting Report* (ICAR), December 13, 2000 [www.icar.ru/eng/newsletter/13.12.2000.html]

Shaw, Sue Olinger, Nina Burakova and Valery Makoukha. 2000. Economic Education in Russia: A Case Study. *S.A.M. Advanced Management Journal* 65:3 (Summer): 29-34.

Tavernise, Sabrina. 2002. U.S. Auditors Find Things Are Different in Russia. *New York Times*, March 12, p. W1.

Vysokov, V. 2000. Center-invest: Banking in Russia using International Accounting Standards. *Euromoney*, Issue 377, September, p. 117.

Williams, Thomas. 2001. Lawyers Pin Hopes on Reforms in Recovering Russia. *International Financial Law Review* 20:11 (November): 34.

Chapter 4

RECENT DEVELOPMENTS IN CORPORATE GOVERNANCE[*]

Abstract

Corporate governance is a new and rapidly changing field in transition economies. Companies must have good corporate governance to attract foreign investment but many Russian firms have governance practices that leave much to be desired. Until a few years ago, transparency was practically unknown and even now many enterprises hide important financial information rather than report it. Minority shareholders often had little or no rights and the value of their investments evaporated as top management plundered the corporation and transferred assets to shell corporations they controlled.

After the Russian default in 1998 several private organizations were formed to protect minority shareholders and to pressure Russian corporations to adopt good corporate governance practices such as electing independent directors, forming an audit committee as part of the board of directors and adopting and i mplementing international f inancial reporting standards. This paper reports on their efforts and discusses how far along Russian corporations are on the road to good corporate governance practices. Some of the information in this paper was gathered from interviews conducted in Moscow and St. Petersburg during the summer of 2003.

INTRODUCTION

Corporate governance has become an important topic in Russia and other transition economies in recent years. Russian directors, owners and corporate managers have started to realize that there are benefits that can accrue from having a good corporate governance structure. Good corporate

---

[*] An earlier version of this chapter was presented at the International Academy of Business and Public Administration Disciplines (IABPAD), Annual Conference, New Orleans, January 23-25, 2004.

governance helps to increase share price and makes it easier to obtain capital. International investors are hesitant to lend money or buy shares in a corporation that does not subscribe to good corporate governance principles. Transparency, independent directors and a separate audit committee are especially important. Some international investors will not seriously consider investing in a company that does not have these things.

Several organizations have popped up in recent years to help adopt and implement good corporate governance principles. The Organisation for Economic Cooperation and Development, the World Bank, the International Finance Corporation, the U.S. Commerce and State Departments and numerous other organizations have been encouraging Russian firms to adopt and implement corporate codes of conduct and good corporate governance principles.

REVIEW OF THE LITERATURE

Hundreds of articles and dozens of books have been written about corporate governance in the last few years alone. One book that should be mentioned is *Corporate Governance* by Monks and Minow (2004). This book is required reading for the ACCA Diploma in Corporate Governance program. Davis Global Advisors publishes an annual *Leading Corporate Governance Indicators*, which measures corporate governance compliance using a variety of indicators.

The Cadbury Report (1992) published the findings of the Committee on Financial Aspects of Corporate Governance. The Greenbury Report (1995) discusses directors' remuneration. The Hampel Committee Report (1998) addresses some of the same issues as the Cadbury and Greenbury reports. It has separate sections on the principles of corporate governance, the role of directors, directors' remuneration, the role of shareholders, accountability and audit and issued conclusions and recommendations. The *Encyclopedia of Corporate Governance* is a good reference tool for obtaining information on corporate governance. It is available online. The OECD's *Principles of Corporate Governance* (1999) has been used as a benchmark for a number of corporate governance codes in transition economies. OECD has also published a *Survey of Corporate Governance Developments in OECD Countries* (2003). The European Corporate Governance Institute maintains many links to codes of corporate conduct for many countries on its website.

Several academic journals are devoted either exclusively or partially to corporate governance issues. The following four journals are devoted exclusively to corporate governance issues:

Corporate Governance: An International Review
Corporate Governance: International Journal of Business in Society
Journal of Management and Governance
Corporate Ownership and Control

Governance is an international monthly newsletter devoted exclusively to corporate governance issues. *Economics of Governance* also publishes articles on corporate governance, in addition to articles on governance in the nonprofit and governmental sectors.

Several websites are also devoted to corporate governance issues and contain many articles, research papers and reports on a wide variety of corporate governance issues. These include:

British Accounting Association Corporate Governance Special Interest Group

Corporate Monitoring

European Corporate Governance Institute

Global Corporate Governance Forum

International Corporate Governance Network

Organisation for Economic Cooperation and Development

World Bank

Within the field of corporate governance literature is a subfield of corporate governance in transition economies. The OECD has published a *White Paper on Corporate Governance in South Eastern Europe* (2003) that is used for guidance by enterprises in that part of the world. This *White Paper* contains sections on shareholder rights and equitable treatment, the role of stakeholders, transparency and disclosure, the responsibilities of the board, and implementation and enforcement. Much of what is contained in this *White Paper* is applicable to corporate governance in Russia as well, although the *White Paper* is not specifically addressed to Russian enterprises.

The OECD website section on corporate governance is subdivided by country. There is a link for Russia that contains studies, papers and announcements pertaining to Russia. One important paper is the OECD's *White Paper on Corporate Governance in Russia* (2002), which contains recommendations for improving corporate governance in Russia. The Russian Corporate Governance Roundtable website also contains documents and announcements pertaining to corporate governance in Russia. The International Finance Corporation, which is affiliated with the World Bank, has a Russia Corporate Governance Project. Its website provides up to date information about several aspects of corporate governance in Russia. The Global Corporate Governance Forum website provides links to more than 60 organizations that are involved in corporate governance issues.

Several Russian organizations also have websites and publication on corporate governance. The Russian Institute of Directors website contains news items as well as publications. Some of its publications and links include a *Code of Corporate Governance* (2002), several Foreign Best Practices Codes and several corporate codes of conduct. They also publish surveys and provide training for corporate directors in Russia. The Independent Directors Association also has a website that provides current information and various documents on corporate governance, mostly pertaining to directors. It also publishes a newsletter, which is available on its website. The Institute of Corporate Law and Corporate Governance also has a website that contains publications about corporate governance in Russia. One of its studies is *Managing Corporate Governance Risks in Russia* (2002). It also provides corporate governance ratings of Russian firms.

Detailed or even brief descriptions of all the papers that have been written on corporate governance in general, corporate governance in transition economies or corporate governance in Russia would take us far afield of the limited focus of the present paper. Citing the sources above is intended to give other researchers some good leads that will aid them in their own research. However, a few papers are worthy of special mention.

Judge, Naoumova and Kutzevol (2003) conducted survey research of Russian managers in December 2002 that found a negative correlation between leadership and firm performance where the same person served as CEO and board chair. This finding is especially curious given the fact that Russian federal legislation has made it illegal since 1996 for the same person to serve as both CEO and board chair at the same time. They also found that the correlation between the proportion of inside directors serving on the board and firm performance becomes increasingly negative the more vigorously a firm pursues a retrenchment strategy. But there was no significant correlation between the proportion of inside directors and firm performance when the firm was not in retrenchment mode, which seems to support the view that inside directors generally fulfill their fiduciary duties to the owners except when their jobs are threatened. Their study complements an earlier study by Wagner, Stimpert and Fubara (1998), which found that very high and very low levels of insider representation on the board had an effect on board performance, whereas moderate levels of representation did not.

Puffer and McCarthy (2003) discuss the substantial progress made in corporate governance in Russia in recent years and track the emergence of corporate governance in Russia through four stages – commercialization, privatization, nomenklatura and statization -- beginning in the mid-1980s. They place special emphasis on problems on nondisclosure and nontransparency that have made Russia one of the riskiest countries for investment. In an earlier work (2002) they examine the question of whether the Russian corporate governance model will evolve into something that looks like the U.S. model or whether it will look more like the European model. They conclude that it will evolve into something that is uniquely Russian, taking into account Russian values, culture and tradition.

Buck (2003) discusses corporate governance in Russia from a historical perspective and the hostile attitude that is taken toward Western and outside investors. He also discusses the persistently strong State influence in Russian corporate governance. Roth and Kostova (2003) tested data from 1,723 firms in 22 countries in Central and Eastern Europe and the Newly Independent States and conclude that cultural factors must be considered when explaining corporate governance in transition economies.

Filatotchev et al (2003) discuss the effect that privatization has had on corporate governance in Eastern and Central European countries. They suggest that excessive management control and ignorance of the governance process is causing problems that could be reduced by increasing the influence of outside directors. Their arguments are supported by case studies.

Peng, Buck and Filatotchev (2003) conducted a survey of 314 privatized Russian firms and tested two hypotheses of agency theory that outside directors and new managers correlate positively to firm performance. They found little support for the hypotheses, a finding that goes against much of the prior research and thinking on this relationship. Their findings question whether this issue must be viewed from other perspectives.

Robertson, Gilley and Street (2003) collected data from 112 U.S. and 74 Russian respondents and looked for patterns of ethical conduct. McCarthy and Puffer (2003) focus on large Russian companies and provide a framework for analyzing corporate governance in transition economies where the corporate governance process is still evolving. They draw on agency theory, stakeholder theory and the cultural embeddedness model in their analysis.

Muravyev (2001) challenges the view that good corporate governance does not exist in Russia and shows through an empirical study that Russian executives can be fired for poor performance. He also challenges the view that the state is a passive shareholder in Russian enterprises and presents evidence of how the ownership of a corporation influences managerial succession.

Filatotchev, Buck and Zhukov (2000) examined enterprises in Russia, Ukraine and Belarus and looked at the relationship between downsizing and outside, noninstitutional shareholding. They found that downsizing is positively correlated with outside, noninstitutional shareholding but that the firm's ability to downsize is negatively correlated with the degree of management shareholding. In other words, when management is entrenched and has a sufficiently large block of voting shares, it can block downsizing in an effort to protect jobs.

METHODOLOGY

Research for this paper began with a review of the literature. When the review was completed, a list of tentative questions was formulated. Experts on corporate governance in Russia were then contacted and interviews were scheduled. Interviews with the following organizations were conducted in July and August 2003:

Deloitte & Touche, Moscow office [www.deloitte.ru]
KPMG, Moscow office [www.kpmg.ru]
KPMG, St. Petersburg office [www.kpmg.ru]
PricewaterhouseCoopers, Moscow office [www.pwcglobal.com/ru]
Ajour, a Russian auditing and consulting firm, Moscow [www.ajour.ru]

PKF (MKD), a Russian audit and consulting firm, St. Petersburg office [www.mcd-pkf.com]

Independent Directors Association, Moscow [www.independentdirector.ru]

This paper incorporates the information gathered during those interviews. The information gathered from these interviews was combined with information that was already published and available. While much of the information gathered during the course of the interviews confirmed what the existing literature already said, much new information was gathered that filled in the gaps in the existing literature and extended and updated prior studies in several important ways.

CORPORATE GOVERNANCE ACTIVITY IN RUSSIA

Corporate governance is in its formative stages in Russia. Like other economies transitioning from a centrally planned economy to a market economy, Russia is going through rapid changes. Transparency in financial reporting is a relatively new concept. The Russian culture and mentality feel more comfortable with secrecy and prefer not to disclose anything they do not have to disclose.

A survey conducted by PricewaterhouseCoopers of transparency in 35 countries ranked Russia number 34, just ahead of China (Haigh 2001). With such a lack of transparency it is little wonder why Russian firms find it so difficult to raise foreign capital. Russia is attempting to overcome this problem by instituting good corporate governance principles such as the appointment of independent directors, establishing audit committees and insisting on more financial disclosure.

Change in the Russian attitude toward transparency and full disclosure is taking place mostly because of the need for foreign capital. Foreign investors hesitate to invest in a company that does not disclose all important financial information. Russian companies found they had to compete for capital in international financial markets and that was the impetus for change.

Some major changes have already taken place, although there is still much work to do. A few private sector organizations have been formed to assist Russian companies upgrade their corporate governance structure to meet international standards. The Russian Institute of Directors and the Independent Directors Association are both engaged in educating Russian directors and monitoring Russian corporations. The International Finance Corporation (IFC), a World Bank funded organization, is devoting substantial resources into its Russia Corporate Governance Project. The Organisation for Economic Cooperation and Development is sponsoring conferences, publishing White Papers and conducting research to help Russian companies upgrade their corporate structures as well. The United States Agency for

International Development (USAID) and other organizations have also supported corporate governance initiatives. The International Trade Administration and the IFC developed a charter of basic principles.

Each of the Big-4 accounting firms – Deloitte & Touche, Ernst & Young, KPMG and PricewaterhouseCoopers -- are also actively engaged in educating corporate directors and top management about the need for good corporate governance. The education process is part of their regular client service. All four firms have newsletters or other kind of educational documents that they distribute to their clients to educate them and keep them up to date on various accounting and corporate governance issues.

The Independent Directors Association (IDA) was formed in 1998, shortly after Russia's financial default. Its stated mission is to establish a community of independent directors. Foreign and Russian investors who used intermediaries to buy shares found their property was disappearing. Brokers and dealers had to do something but they didn't know what to do. One option was to sue, using the class action approach but this option did not exist in Russia. Also, lawsuits are not an efficient way of recovering property in Russia. The Independent Directors Association was developed as a vehicle to protect investors. It is a coordination center.

IDA pushed for the election of independent directors to represent minority shareholders. It advocated unanimous voting on corporate boards so that even one dissenting vote could prevent a measure from passing. The large Russian corporations balked at this provision, since they thought such a provision would result in having their corporation run by minority shareholders. Gasprom, a state owned monopoly, was especially vigorous in its opposition to this provision.

The IDA has also been pushing for Russian corporate boards to have subcommittees to perform various functions. Having subcommittees like a compensation committee or an audit committee is a new concept for many Russian companies but one they are not opposed to. The IDA has been pushing to have the audit committee composed exclusively of independent directors. There is some external pressure for Russian companies to have independent directors, especially on the audit committee. The New York Stock Exchange has given nonresident companies two years to comply with NYSE rules as a condition of having their stock listed on its exchange. One of its requirements is to have independent directors on the audit committee. One important factor investors look at when determining whether to invest in a Russian company is whether the company has independent directors. If it does not, the company is much less attractive as a potential investment.

As a coordination vehicle, the IDA acts as a facilitator. It brings interested parties together and disseminates information. At the time of the interview, it had 30 investment banks and hedge funds as members. As of September 2003 it opened up membership to corporations as well. It also has contacts with each of the Big-4 accounting firms as well as smaller accounting firms and representatives of the various Russian stock exchanges.

It has also formed a relationship with the National Association of Corporate Directors in the United States. The IDA also gives awards each year for the company with the best financial statements. The award looks at disclosure and transparency, not the bottom line or financial ratios.

The New York Stock Exchange and the London exchange are the two main targets for Russian companies in need of foreign capital. The IDA has established a relationship with both of these exchanges as well as Standard & Poors. Whether Russian companies issue financial statements using U.S. Generally Accepted Accounting Principles (GAAP) or International Accounting Standards (IAS) depends on which of the two exchanges they are targeting. Companies that want to raise capital in the United States tend to prepare GAAP statements, whereas those that want to raise capital in London tend to issue IAS statements.

In the last few years there has been a shift away from GAAP statements toward IAS statements. The reason given in the interviews was that in a post-Enron world, U.S. accounting standards are seen as being of lower quality or less reliability than International Accounting Standards. Since the Russian Finance Ministry has ordered Russian companies to adopt IAS effective January 1, 2004 (one year before the EU), this trend away from GAAP statements is likely to continue. However, GAAP statements may not disappear altogether from Russian company financial reports. Russian companies that are affiliates of a U.S. company are still likely to prepare financial statements based on U.S. GAAP, since it is more likely to try to raise capital at one of the New York stock exchanges than the London exchange.

Standard & Poor's initiated a pilot project out of its London office to measure the extent to which Russian companies complied with certain corporate governance attributes. It chose five Russian companies and scored them based on a variety of factors. The four key components the S&P study scored were:
- Ownership structure;
- Relations with shareholders and shareholder rights provisions;
- Financial transparency and information disclosure; and
- The structure of the board of directors. (Feinberg 2000)

It used the following 16 corporate governance criteria to arrive at the scores for each company:
1. Ownership structure and influence;
2. Transparency of ownership;
3. Concentration and influence of ownership;
4. Financial stakeholder relations;
5. Regularity of, ease of, access to, and information on shareholder meetings;
6. Voting and shareholder meeting procedures;
7. Ownership rights (registration and transferability, equality of ownership rights);

8. Financial transparency and information disclosure;
9. Type of public disclosure standards adopted;
10. Timing of, and access to, public disclosure;
11. Independence and standing of auditor;
12. Board and management structure and process;
13. Board structure and composition;
14. Role and effectiveness of board;
15. Role and independence of outside directors; and
16. Board and executive compensation, evaluation and succession policies. (Anon. 2000/2001)

The Standard and Poor's study came about partly because of the McKinsey & Co. Investor Opinion Study of June 2000, which concluded that:
"Three quarters of investors say board practices are at least as important to them as financial performance when they are evaluating companies for investment, especially in emerging markets ... Over 80% of investors say they would be prepared to pay more for the shares of well-governed companies than those of poorly governed companies." (Anon. 2000/2001)

The methodology it used could also be applied to companies in other countries, making it possible to compare a Russian company to a company in a developed market economy. The pilot project proved to be so successful that S&P plans to expand it to rate companies worldwide based on their adherence to corporate governance principles.

WEAKNESSES IN CORPORATE GOVERNANCE

Russia has a well earned reputation for poor corporate governance. As of 2001, the largest Russian companies still hid their assets and cash flow from minority shareholders. Gazprom, Russia's largest company, ignores the legal requirement of an independent audit. Lukoil, Russia's largest oil company, routinely issues its financial statements months beyond promised deadlines, and when it finally did issue some financial statements, they were unaudited statements covering just a six-month period rather than the full year statements that investors were expecting. (Anon. 2001a).

Various private groups have issued codes of corporate governance that set out principles to be followed by boards and corporate officers. These codes provide guidance and attempt to raise the ethical quality of Russian executives to that of Western company executives. The Russian Duma has passed laws tightening up corporate governance requirements. But laws and voluntary (or even mandatory) codes of corporate conduct are not enough. Merely making rules and laws will not necessarily result in good actions by board members. Rules are useless without ethics. One of the positive aspects of the Code of Corporate Conduct that was prepared under the direction of the Federal Commission for the Securities Market (FCSM) is that ethics are stressed. The Code is imbued with ethics (Metzger et al. 2002).

Merely passing laws is not enough, either. A study by Pistor, Raiser and Gelfer (2000) concluded that the effectiveness of legal institutions is much more important than having good laws on the books. Transplanting Western laws into transition economies and having extensive legal reforms are not sufficient to strengthen corporate governance, although such things are necessary. Even passing Russian laws is not always effective at changing corporate governance practices. Judge, Naoumova and Kutzevol (2003) point out that a number of Russian companies have the same person installed as board chair and CEO, a practice that has been illegal in Russia since 1996.

However, there is some evidence that good practices are taking hold in Russian corporations. A study by Muravyev (2001) found that it is possible to get rid of ineffective managers. His study examined 419 medium-size and large Russian enterprises having between 100 and 5,000 employees in six manufacturing industries. He looked at the replacement of general directors over an 18-month period. His study found that about 18 percent of top management was replaced during the period and that about 40 percent of all new directors were outsiders. About 65 percent of them were fired for poor performance while 35 percent left for other reasons. Table 1 shows top executive turnover for the period under study.

Table 1
Top Executive Turnover in Sampled Companies
January 1999 – May 2000

	Number of Firms	%
Total responses	413	100
Did not change general director	337	82
Changed general director	76	18
Changed general director for outsider	30	7
Changed general director for insider	46	11

Source: Muravyev (2001)

Muravyev (2001) also found that the ownership structure strongly influences management turnover. As might be expected, turnover is less in firms where insiders have a controlling interest. Table 2 shows the relationship of insider ownership to management turnover.

Table 2
Insider Ownership and Replacement of General Directors
(end-1999)

Insider Share %	Number of Firms	Firms Changing General Director	% of Total Firms
From 0 to 25	68	23	34
From 25 to 50	79	25	32
From 50 to 75	62	9	15
From 75 to 100	153	11	7
Total	362	68	19

Source: Muravyev (2001)

Muravyev (2001) also found that managers tended to be replaced more frequently at weaker performing firms and that there was a higher probability of replacement where outsiders had more influence. He concludes that corporate governance of large and medium-size firms is not completely inefficient in Russia.

Filatotchev, Buck and Zhukov (2000) conducted a study that supports some of the Muravyev findings. They found a positive correlation between the proportion of outside shareholding and the ability to downsize and found that the ability to downsize was reduced as the percentage of shares owned by insiders increased, a finding that is consistent with the management entrenchment theory.

PROTECTING SHAREHOLDERS

Shareholders in every country are in need of protection, but especially so in Russia and other transition economies that have not yet established a strong rule of law and corporate legal principles that protect shareholders, especially minority shareholders. Until a few years ago, minority shareholders were not only totally ignored but actually abused by the Russian companies they owned shares in. It was a common practice for Russian companies to manipulate shareholder registries or even erase their names from the corporate registry (Metzger et al. 2002) and funnel money into an intricate web of shell companies, thus depriving minority shareholders of cash flow. Management would sell off assets to entities they controlled indirectly, depriving minority shareholders of value (Iskyan 2002). Such practices became less severe after the Russian Duma enacted legislation to protect minority shareholders, but it would be premature to say that such practices have stopped altogether. The rule of law is still weak in Russia. It is difficult to protect property rights in a country where property rights did not exist for three generations.

THE INDEPENDENT DIRECTOR CODE

As was previously mentioned, a number of corporate governance codes have been developed in the last few years, both by international organizations and by Russian organizations. The Independent Director Code is one of them. This code was developed by the Independent Directors Association jointly with the Russian Institute of Directors in partnership with Moscow Interbank Currency Exchange, the International Finance Corporation and the Good Governance Program of the International Trade Administration of the U.S. Department of Commerce.

RUSSIAN CODE OF CORPORATE CONDUCT

The Russian Institute of Directors (RID) issued the final version of its Corporate Governance Code in April 2002. Although Russian law deals with many aspects of corporate governance, the laws that are on the books were considered to be inadequate to deal with certain issues that are not of a legal nature. Furthermore, it was recognized that the law should not try to address all issues relating to corporate governance, since some things legitimately lie outside of the law, such as private contract and management issues. Also, the legal system is not designed to respond to rapidly changing conditions. Thus, the need was felt for a corporate governance code to provide the needed guidance.

The Code contains a list of recommendations for best practices and incorporates many of the recommendations included in various OECD publications. Chapter 1 states that corporate governance should be based on respect for the rights and lawful interests of all participants and mentions trust as a primary ingredient of good corporate management. In the past, shareholders at some Russian companies have found it difficult or impossible to exercise their rights. The Code states that shareholders should be provided with the means of registering their shares and they should also be given the opportunity to quickly dispose of them. Shareholders should be notified of shareholder meetings and should be able to attend. They should be able to easily vote their shares. Sec. 1.4 states that shareholders should have the right to receive regular and timely information about the company. This can be accomplished by:

- providing shareholders with comprehensive information on each item of the agenda in preparation for a general shareholders meeting;
- providing information that is sufficient for evaluating the results of operations, such as an annual report; and
- establishing the position of corporate secretary, whose job it will be to ensure that shareholders have access to information about the company.

Such provisions may seem bland and obvious to readers from developed market economies, but the reason why such provisions were included in the very first chapter of the Code was because of the widespread abuse of shareholders in regard to exercising shareholder rights and having access to corporate information.

Chapter 2 addresses the rules and procedures that should exist regarding the general shareholders meeting. Procedures for holding a shareholders meeting must be put in place and shareholders must be treated fairly and given the opportunity to participate in such meetings. At least 30 days notice should be given before every meeting, even though the law requires that only 20 days notice be given. The notice should contain sufficient information to allow shareholders to make informed decisions regarding the issues and to decide whether, and to what extent they shall participate. Agenda items should be stated clearly so that there is no misinterpretation as to their meaning. Meetings should be held at times and places that are convenient for shareholders. There are rules about quorums and what to do if a company has a large number of small shareholders.

Chapter 3 addresses issues relating to the duties of the board of directors. The Board is supposed to provide efficient supervision of the company's financial and business operations, safeguard and protect the rights of shareholders and help resolve corporate conflicts. There are three categories of director – executive, non-executive and independent. An independent director is one who:

- has not been an officer or employee of the corporation for at least three years;
- is not an officer of another company in which any company officer is a member of the appointments and remuneration committee of the board;
- is not affiliated with the company's managing organization;
- is not bound by certain contractual obligations with the company;
- is not a major business partner of the company; and
- is not a representative of the government.

There are also provisions prohibiting the gainful use of insider information, provisions discussing the duties of the audit committee and the ethics committee and the liability of board members.

Chapter 4 discusses executive bodies of the company, which are charged with managing the company's current affairs, making them responsible for attaining the company's objectives and goals and implementing the company's strategies and policies. Chapter 5 outlines the duties and responsibilities of the corporate secretary. The secretary is responsible for preparing and holding the shareholders' meeting as well as for a wide range of other activities involving shareholders.

Chapter 6 is about major corporate actions that result in fundamental corporate changes, such as a change in the rights of shareholders, reorganizations, acquisitions and liquidation. Chapter 7 addresses issues relating to disclosure about the company. The enterprise's policy should guarantee low cost and unhampered access to information. A great deal is said about the forms that disclosure should take. There are discussions about the information that should be included in the annual and quarterly reports and about the necessity to disclose all relevant information to shareholders in a timely manner. The annual report should include:

- the company's position in the industry;
- attainment of the firm's strategic objectives;
- annual results, both actual and planned;
- prospects for the company's development, which includes discussions of sales, productivity, market share, income generation, profitability and the debt/equity ratio;
- major risk factors;
- relations with competitors; and
- review of the company's most significant transactions during the prior year.

Chapter 8 discusses supervision of company's financial and business operations. There are sections on the organization of activity of the audit committee, the actual audit and the need for an independent, certified audit. Chapter 9 discusses dividends and dividend policy and suggests that the company implement a transparent and easily understood mechanism for determining the amount of dividends to be paid and the payment strategy. Chapter 10 discusses the resolution of corporate conflicts.

The interviews revealed that corporate codes of conduct are becoming increasingly popular. One might think that adopting a corporate code of conduct would be a major positive step, which it well may be. However, the interviews also revealed that many corporations either do not have a corporate code of conduct or, if they do have one, tend to ignore it. Adopting such codes is sometimes seen as a public relations gimmick, something to be brought out and displayed to the financial community, but not something that can be referred to and used to manage or guide the corporation. If this is true, it means that much must be done before substantive change can be achieved.

CORPORATE GOVERNANCE SURVEY

In September 2003 the Russian Institute of Directors (RID 2003) published the results of a survey conducted by the Federal Commission for the Securities Market of the Russian Federation (FCSM), the Institute of the Securities Market and Management (ISMM), and the Tacis project, "Capital Market Investment Advisory Services" (INVAS). The survey consisted of a questionnaire returned by more than 60 of Russia's largest joint stock companies. A number of interesting facts were uncovered.

Most corporate boards in developed market economies have subcommittees that are assigned certain tasks. Some of the most common board subcommittees are for audit, nominations and remuneration. The survey found that Russian companies still do not have such subcommittees, as a general rule. Only one Russian company has a permanent committee on strategic development, for example.

The large Russian firms have an acceptable mix of executive directors and non-executive directors, many of which are truly independent directors. The ratio of executive to external directors was about 30:70, which is in line with the Russian Federation law on joint stock companies as well as with western best practices recommendations. More than half of the companies (52%) have independent directors on the board. The ratio of dependent to independent directors is about 80:20. Independent directors account for less than 30% of all external directors. Most codes of best practices call for a majority of external directors to be independent, which means that the concept of having a strong representation of independent directors has not yet taken root in Russia's corporate mentality.

Assessing board and management effectiveness should be part of every company's policy. Yet less than 2 percent of the large Russian corporations have any formal process for assessing board effectiveness. About 11 percent of the companies have developed a process but have not yet implemented it, while 87 percent have no formal assessment procedures at all. Interestingly enough, the vast majority of the companies that responded to the survey regard their corporate governance as good (81%) to excellent (11%).

More than three out of four corporate boards have between 6 and 10 members. Table 3 shows the breakdown by size.

Table 3
Size of Corporate Boards

Members	%
1 to 5	4
6 to 10	77
11 to 15	15
16 or more	4

More than two out of three board members devote between one and five days a month to board activities. Table 4 shows the breakdown in terms of time spent on board activities.

Table 4
Time Spend on Board Activities

Days per Month	%
1 to 5	68
6 to 10	26
11 to 15	0
More than 15	6

An important function of every corporate board is strategic planning. Although top management also plays a role, it is important for the board to also be involved in strategic planning. The survey found that all boards are involved in strategic planning, although some boards play a more active role than others. Table 5 provides a summary on the degree of board involvement in strategic planning.

Table 5
Board Involvement in Strategic Planning

	%
Board members take an active part in development of the company strategy; plan strategy is officially approved by the board.	36
Board initiates and manages development of plan and strategy and officially approves	33
Board contributes to strategy development during discussions at meetings and formally approves it.	16
The plan is developed by the management; board approves it.	15
Board is not involved in the development of the plan; it participates in consultations on ad-hoc basis.	0

Risk management is not something that corporations are overly concerned with, according to the survey. Only 11 percent of the boards take part in the development of risk management policy. In the vast majority of cases it lets management take care of this responsibility. Table 6 shows the amount of board involvement in risk management. For some unexplained reason the sum is more than 100 percent.

Table 6
Board Involvement in Risk Management

	%
Board takes part in development of risk management policy	11
Board contributes to development of risk management policy by discussing risk issues at one or several meetings.	28
Basic approaches to risk management are developed by company management; the board formally approves them.	11
Board is not formally involved in risk management policy development; board takes part in consultations on ad-hoc questions.	51

Disclosure remains a big problem for Russian companies. There is a tendency not to disclose information, for a variety of reasons. During Soviet times, disclosure was minimal because there was no one to disclose anything to and all enterprises were owned by the state. Also, government and government officials were distrusted and government employees preferred not to disclose any more information than what the government bureaucracy demanded. With the advent of the market economy after three generations of communist rule, secrecy is deeply imbedded into the Russian mentality. Also, Russian managers are afraid that disclosing anything about the business with increase their taxes or provide their competitors with information they can use to reduce their company's market share. Not surprisingly, the survey showed that most corporate boards do not show much of a predisposition for disclosing corporate information, in spite of pressure from the OECD, various corporate codes and other organizations to provide more disclosure. Table 7 provides some details regarding disclosure involvement by corporate boards.

Table 7
Board Role in Overseeing Disclosure and Communications

	%
Board assists regular contacts with shareholders and other concerned parties	13
Board approves all press releases and other official statements on most important issues	2
Board provides general control of information disclosures and communication with shareholders	44
Board discusses related ad-hoc issues	27
Board formally approves information policy, which is developed and implemented by the company	15

Companies were asked some questions about director compensation. Director compensation is a sensitive issue in Russia, so the questionnaire did not ask specific questions about level of compensation, but it did ask about the various forms of compensation board members receive. Table 8 shows the results of the survey.

Table 8
Forms of Director Compensation

Forms of Compensation	%
Compensation of expenses related to fulfilling director functions	53
Fixed compensation	58
Bonuses	9
Participation in profits	9
Stock options	0
Other	12

It is interesting that stock options are not used to compensate directors at any of the large Russian enterprises that responded to the survey. Stock options are a common form of compensation in western firms. Compensation for executives followed a similar pattern, with no firms using stock options as a form of compensation. Table 9 shows the breakdown of executive compensation by category.

Table 9
Forms of Executive Compensation

Forms of Compensation	%
Fixed compensation (salary)	71
Bonuses	66
Participation in profits	13
Stock options	0
Other	5

Participants were asked to assign scores to a series of questions involving problems of corporate board activity. Scores ranged from 1 to 5, with 5 being the most important Table 10 shows the average scores for each category.

Table 10
Most Important Problems in Board Activities

	Average Score
Effective participation of board in corporate strategy development	4.1
Effective control of board over the strategy implementation	4.0
Establishing relations with shareholders, investors and authorities	3.9
Effective control over the activities of the executive body	3.7
Provision of integrity of accounting and financial reporting systems	3.5
Effective management recruitment policy provisions	3.4
Provision of effective board member nominating policy	3.3
Development and provision of an effective internal control system	3.2
Introduction of effective senior management compensation policy	3.2
Provision of external auditor independence	3.1
Provision of law maintenance	3.1
Increase effectiveness of the current board staff	3.1
Development of an effective risk monitoring and management system	3.0
Provision of an effective information disclosure system	3.0
Carrying out regular senior management evaluation procedures	3.0

Introduction of effective board members compensation policy	2.8
Carrying out regular board activity evaluation procedures	2.8

The most important problem according to the respondents was to have effective board participation in the development of corporate strategy. Of almost equal importance was the effective control of the board over strategy implementation. Establishing relations with shareholders, investors and authorities was also very important. Among the least important problems were introducing an effective board member compensation policy and carrying out regular board activity evaluation procedures.

Respondents were also asked to assess the importance of various skills that are essential for board member effectiveness. The most important skill was strategic planning, followed by decision making methods and procedures, corporate law, negotiation skills, financial analysis, business planning and business plan evaluation, investor relations and company restructuring. Table 11 shows the breakdown ranked by importance.

Table 11
Importance of Various Skills

	Average Score
Strategic planning	4.7
Decision making methods and procedures	4.3
Corporate law	4.3
Negotiation skills	4.3
Financial analysis	4.3
Company restructuring	4.2
Investor relations	4.2
Business planning and business plan evaluation	4.2
Conflict management	4.1
Risk management	4.0
Marketing	4.0
Board activity management	3.9
Top management recruitment strategies	3.9
Macroeconomic analysis	3.9
Project management	3.9
Personnel motivation	3.8
Board relations and corporate ethics	3.7
Mergers and acquisitions	3.7
Public relations	3.5

Board and executive management effectiveness is a very important element of good corporate governance. Companies should have detailed procedures to determine the extent of management and board effectiveness. The survey revealed that the vast majority of companies do not have any formal procedures to evaluate effectiveness. Table 12 provides a summary of company policies in this regard by category for board effectiveness. Table 13 does the same thing for management effectiveness.

Table 12
Assessment of Board Effectiveness

	%
The company has assessment criteria, employs formal assessment procedures of board member activities	2
The company has developed (or is developing) board activity assessment procedures but they are not employed	11
The company has no formal procedures	87

Table 13
Assessment of Management Effectiveness

	%
The company has assessment criteria, employs formal assessment procedures of top management activities	26
The company has developed (or is developing) top management activity assessment procedures but they are not employed	12
The company has no formal procedures	62

Interestingly enough, the vast majority of respondents think they have good to excellent corporate governance. Table 14 shows the breakdown by category.

Table 14
Self-Assessment of Own Corporate Governance Practices by Companies

	%
Excellent	11
Good in general but needs improvement	81
Unsatisfactory	4
Difficult to say	4

Obviously, the perception of the Russian respondents is different than the perception of observers from developed market economies. Whereas observers from developed market economies would be quick to say that there is much room for improvement, or even that Russian corporate governance is in a state of crisis, the Russians themselves do not see that corporate governance for their company poses much of a problem. Perhaps that is a good thing, since seeing their corporation through the eyes of someone from the west might make them depressed. But on the other hand, if there is a widespread perception that only minor changes need to be made to their corporation's corporate governance structure, it is quite possible that progress will be slow because they see the situation as not requiring emergency assistance.

Having said that, it should also be mentioned that all of the respondents thought that corporate governance needs to be improved in Russia. Table 15 gives the statistical breakdown.

Table 15
Necessity of Improving
Corporate Governance in Russia

	%
Vitally important	80
Important	20
Not important	0

CONCLUDING COMMENTS

Russian financial statements still suffer from a lack of transparency. It is difficult to overcome generations of Russian culture and the Russian mentality, which prefers secrecy to disclosure. But the trend is toward more transparency, more independent directors and financial statements that have a degree of international credibility.

Poor corporate governance policies cause the shares of Russian firms to sell for $54 billion less than they would if their companies had good corporate governance policies, according to James Fenkner of Troika Dialog, Russia's largest brokerage firm (Anon. 2001a). Bernard Black, using data from Troika, conducted a study to determine whether corporate governance matters, in terms of share price. He found that it made a huge difference (Black 2001). Likewise, Russian companies that improved their corporate governance practices by adopting and implementing the Corporate Governance Code saw their share prices increase (Miller 2002).

However, much still needs to be done. It is difficult to superimpose a corporate code of conduct on the Russian culture, especially if the code is drawn up by foreigners. Codes of conduct and the corporate governance policies they espouse will only take a firm hold in Russia when a significant number of Russian directors and managers actually believe that having and utilizing such codes is the right thing to do. The survey showed that Russian companies are on the right track, although much remains to be done.

REFERENCES

Anonymous. 2001a. Minority What? *Economist*, 358(8210), 72 (February 24).

Anonymous. (December 2000/January 2001). S&P Devises Scoring System for Corporate Governance Risk. *Central European* 10(10), 20-21.

Black, B. 2001. Does Corporate Governance Matter? A Crude Test Using Russian Data, *University of Pennsylvania Law Review* 149(6), 2131-2150 (June).

British Accounting Association Corporate Governance Special Interest Group website http://www.baacgsig.qub.ac.uk/

Buck, T. 2003. Modern Russian Corporate Governance: Convergent Forces or Product of Russia's History? *Journal of World Business*, 38(4), 299-313.

Cadbury, A., et al. 1992. (The Cadbury Report) *Report of the Committee on Financial Aspects of Corporate Governance* (December 1), London: Gee Publishing Ltd... Available at http://www.worldbank.org/html/fpd/privatesector/cg/docs/cadbury.pdf.

Corporate Monitoring http://www.corpmon.com/

Davis Global Advisors. *Leading Corporate Governance Indicators,* Newton, MA: Davis Global Advisors. Annual publication. http://www.davisglobal.com/publications/lcgi/index.html

Encyclopedia of Corporate Governance http://www.encycogov.com/

European Corporate Governance Institute website http://www.ecgi.org/

European Corporate Governance Institute link to Codes http://www.ecgi.org/codes/all_codes.htm

Feinberg, P. 2000. Historically Indifferent Russia Starts to Heed Corporate Governance Rules, *Pensions & Investments*, 28(23), 18-19 (November 13).

Filatotchev, I., Buck, T. and Zhukov, V. 2000. Downsizing in Privatized Firms in Russia, Ukraine, and Belarus. *Academy of Management Journal*, 43(3), 286-304.

Filatotchev, I., Wright, M., Uhlenbruck, K., Tihanyi, L., and Hoskisson, R. 2003. Governance, Organizational Capabilities, and Restructuring in Transition Economies. *Journal of World Business*, 38(4), 331-347.

Global Corporate Governance Forum http://www.gcgf.org/

Greenbury, R. et al. 1995. (Greenbury Report). *Directors' Remuneration: Report of a Study Group Chaired by Sir Richard Greenbury*, (July 17), London: Gee Publishing Ltd. Available at http://www.baacgsig.qub.ac.uk/

Haigh, A. 2001. We View Russia's Future with Optimism. *Kommersant-Daily* (January 26) [www.pwcglobal.ru/].

Hampel Committee. 1998. *Hampel Committee Report*, (January), London: Gee Publishing Ltd. Available at
   http://www.ecgi.org/codes/country_documents/uk/hampel_index.htm
Independent Directors Association website www.independentdirector.ru
Independent Directors Association. 2003. *Independent Director Code* (April 15 Draft), Moscow: Independent Directors Association. Available at www.independentdirector.ru.
Institute of Corporate Law and Corporate Governance website www.iclg.ru
Institute of Corporate Law and Corporate Governance. 2002. *Managing Corporate Governance Risks in Russia* (May), Moscow: Institute of Corporate Law and Corporate Governance.
International Corporate Governance Network website http://www.icgn.org/
International Finance Corporation, Russia Corporate Governance Project website http://www2.ifc.org/rcgp/english.htm
Iskyan, K. 2002. Clean-up Time in Russia, *Global Finance* 32-35 (February).
Judge, W.Q., Naoumova, I. & Kutzevol, N. 2003. *Corporate Governance in Russia: An Empirical Study of Russian Managers' Perception*. Paper presented at the Gorbachev Foundation Conference on Corporate Governance in Transition Economies held at Northeastern University, Boston, April 2003. Published in *Journal of World Business*, 38(4), 385-396 (November 2003) under the title Corporate Governance and Firm Performance in Russia: An Empirical Study.
McCarthy, D.J. and Puffer, S.M. 2003. Corporate Governance in Russia: A Framework for Analysis. *Journal of World Business*, 38(4), 397-415.
McCarthy, D.J. and Puffer, S.M. 2002. Corporate Governance in Russia: Towards a European, US, or Russian Model? *European Management Journal*, 20(6), 630-641.
Metzger, B., Dean, R.N. and Bloom, D. 2002. Russia's Code of Corporate Conduct: An Innovative Approach to Solving Shareholder Rights Abuses, *The Corporate Governance Advisor*10 (2), 12-17 (March/April).
Miller, S. 2002. Law and Order Makes its Mark, *Banker* 152(913), 44-45 (March).
Monks, R. A.G. & Minow, N. (Eds) 2004. *Corporate Governance*, third edition, London: Blackwell Publishers.
Muravyev, A. 2001. Turnover of Top Executives in Russian Companies. *Russian Economic Trends*, 10(1), 20-24.
National Association of Corporate Directors website
   http://www.nacdonline.org/
Organisation for Economic Cooperation and Development website http://www.oecd.org/document/62/0,2340,en_2649_37439_1912830_1_1_1_37439,00.html
Organisation for Economic Cooperation and Development. 2003. *White Paper on Corporate Governance in South Eastern Europe*, Paris: OECD. www.oecd.org.

Organisation for Economic Cooperation and Development. 2003. *Survey of Corporate Governance Developments in OECD Countries*, Paris: OECD.

Organisation for Economic Cooperation and Development. 2002. *White Paper on Corporate Governance in Russia*, (April 15), Paris: OECD. Available at http://www.oecd.org/dataoecd/10/3/2789982.pdf.

Organisation for Economic Cooperation and Development. 1999. *Principles of Corporate Governance*, Paris: OECD. Available at http://www.oecd.org/dataoecd/47/50/4347646.pdf.

Peng, M., Buck, T. and Filatotchev, I. 2003. Do Outside Directors and New Managers Help Improve Firm Performance? An Exploratory Study in Russian Privatization. *Journal of World Business*, 38(4), 348-360.

Pistor, K., Raiser, M. and Gelfer, S. 2000. Law and Finance in Transition Economies, *Economics of Transition* 8(2), 325-368.

Puffer, S.M. and McCarthy, D.J. 2003. The Emergence of Corporate Governance in Russia. *Journal of World Business*, 38(4), 284-298.

Robertson, C.J., Gilley, K.M., and Street, M.D. 2003. The Relationship between Ethics and Firm Practices in Russia and the United States. *Journal of World Business*, 38(4), 375-384.

Roth, K. and Kostova, T. 2003. Organizational Coping with Institutional Upheaval in Transition Economies. *Journal of World Business*, 38(4), 314-330.

Russian Corporate Governance Roundtable website http://www.corp-gov.org/

Russian Institute of Directors website www.rid.ru

Russian Institute of Directors. 2003. *Structure and Activities of Boards of Directors of Russian Joint-Stock Companies*. Moscow: Russian Institute of Directors. www.rid.ru

Russian Institute of Directors. 2002. *Corporate Governance Code* (April 5), Moscow: Russian Institute of Directors, www.rid.ru.

Wagner, J., Stimpert, J., & Fubara, E. 1998. Board Composition and Organizational Performance: Two Studies of Insider/Outsider Effects. *Journal of Management Studies*, 35(5), 655-677.

World Bank Corporate Governance website http://www.worldbank.org/html/fpd/privatesector/cg/

Chapter 5

PROBLEMS OF FOREIGN DIRECT INVESTMENT IN RUSSIA*

Abstract
More than 100 countries are competing for foreign direct investment. One of the factors that adversely affects the ability to attract foreign capital is the lack of credibility of reported financial information. This barrier is especially prevalent in transition economies, since they have not developed the financial reporting infrastructure that developed countries already enjoy. Adopting International Accounting Standards (IAS) or their successor, International Financial Reporting Standards (IFRS), is seen as one way to overcome this barrier and many transition economies are adopting or have already adopted IFRS as a means of giving credibility to corporate financial statements. All of the former Soviet republics have made some attempt to have their enterprises convert to IFRS. Some have been more successful than others, for a variety of reasons. This paper focuses on Russia's attempt to adopt IFRS and the problems Russian firms face with the adoption and implementation of IFRS.

INTRODUCTION

Perhaps Frits Bolkestein, European Commissioner for the Internal Market, sums it up best when, referring to the adoption of International Financial Reporting Standards (IFRS), he says that:
> "investors and other stakeholders will be able to compare like with like. It will help European firms to compete on equal terms when raising capital on world markets." (BDO et al 2002)

---

* An earlier version of this chapter was presented at the Thirteenth International Conference of the International Trade & Finance Association, Vaasa, Finland, May 28-31, 2003.

He might just as easily have said Russian firms rather than European firms. More than 100 countries are competing for foreign direct investment. One of the factors that adversely affect the ability to attract foreign capital is the lack of credibility of reported financial information. This barrier is especially prevalent in transition economies, since they have not developed the financial reporting infrastructure that developed countries already enjoy. Adopting International Financial Reporting Standards (IFRS) is seen as one way to overcome this barrier and many transition economies are adopting or have already adopted IFRS as a means of giving credibility to corporate financial statements. Adoption will also have a beneficial effect on the cost of capital and will lead to a degree of cultural convergence (Damant 1999).

The Eurasian Association of Accountants and Auditors suggested that transition economies adopt International Financial Reporting Standards (IFRS) for the following reasons (ICAR May/June 2001):

- IFRS are aimed at providing the transparency of accounting and reflecting the real economic situation, which will enable users of financial statements to make the right decisions.
- In developing IFRS, experts use the best internationally recognized principles. That is why International Financial Reporting Standards are logically clear from the economic standpoint.
- IFRS are sufficiently simple to be understood by all users of financial statements worldwide who have the adequate knowledge of business, economics, accounting and finance.

Vorushkin (2001) gives the following reasons why Russian firms should adopt IFRS. Some reasons have more to do with managerial efficiency than transparency.

- The preparation of group accounts would be cheaper and quicker because all segments of the enterprise would be using the same accounting system rather than different systems, which is the way many Russian firms now operate.
- Accounting expertise within Russian multinationals would become transferable between subsidiaries in different countries.
- Internal control will improve because the enterprise would operate in a standardized environment.
- Firms could obtain improved access to funds and lower cost of capital because of increased transparency and the harmonization of standards.
- The cost of upgrading and training in accounting software would be reduced because IFRS rules change less frequently than the more volatile Russian Accounting Standards (RAS).
- Adopting IFRS would provide less scope for management abuses and minority shareholder rights would be better protected.
- Establish equal and trustworthy international business relationships because foreign firms feel more comfortable dealing with Russian companies that use the same accounting principles.

• Make better management decisions that are based on economic reality, which will result in the more efficient use of capital.

While there are many good reasons for adopting accounting standards that are recognized internationally, there are also problems or impediments involved in adopting such standards. A survey of partners of the six largest accounting firms in 59 countries found the following impediments to achieving IFRS convergence:

Concerns Expressed about Impediments to Achieving IFRS Convergence Survey of Six Large Accounting Firms in 59 Countries

Problems Mentioned	Percent of respondents
Complicated nature of particular standards	51
Tax-driven nature of the national accounting regime	47
Disagreement with certain significant IFRS	39
Insufficient guidance for first-time application of IFRS	35
Limited capital markets	30
Satisfaction with national accounting standards among investors/users	21
Translation difficulties	18

Source: BDO et al (2002), p. 10.

Transparent financial information is a crucial factor in achieving economic growth and stability (Radoutsky 2001) and adopting IFRS is seen as a way to achieve the level of transparency needed to satisfy the information needs of the international investor market. A report issued by the European Bank for Reconstruction and Development in October 2000 stated that it is impossible to assess the performance of large enterprises in need of restructuring because of a lack of financial statements prepared in accordance with IFRS (ICAR Nov/Dec 2000a).

One would think that countries that have transparent financial reporting standards like those incorporated in IFRS would have higher growth rates than countries that do not have transparent standards, all other things being equal (Larson and York 1996). Studies have shown this to be the case. However, one study (Larson 1993) that included data from 35 African countries found that growth rates were significantly higher for countries that adopt and modify IFRS than for countries that either adopted IFRS without modification or did not adopt IFRS. It is not clear why this is the case, since many factors are involved in a country's economic growth (Arndt 1987; Bauer 1991, 1976; Lal 2001, 1986; Hanke and Walters 1991). It would be interesting to see the result if someone replicated the Larson study, using data from the countries of the former Soviet Union and Eastern Europe.

ADOPTING IFRS

All of the former Soviet republics have made some attempt to have their enterprises convert to IFRS. Some have been more successful than others, for a variety of reasons. However, merely adopting IFRS is not enough. They must be implemented and the audits of companies that adopt IFRS must be sufficiently strong to foster confidence in the international investment community (ICAR March/April 2001a). On July 25, 2002 Russia's Prime Minister Mikhail Kasyanov announced that all Russian companies and banks must prepare their financial statements in accordance with IFRS starting January 1, 2004. In March 2001 the European Union gave a 2 million euro grant to enhance the competence of Russian auditors and to support audit regulation reform aimed at making local companies more transparent (ICAR March/April 2001b) This paper focuses on Russia's attempt to adopt IFRS and the problems Russian firms face with the adoption and implementation of IFRS.

The Russian economy needs foreign investment to ensure a high and stable rate of growth. But the lack of transparency of most Russian companies creates risks for potential investors and reduces the attractiveness of investing in the Russian economy, thus placing an obstacle in the way of foreign investment and financial inflows. Informational transparency, based on trustworthy, timely corporate financial statements that use International Financial Reporting Standards (IFRS) and principles, and that are verified by independent qualified audits, is one of the most important components of corporate governance, the mission of which is, first of all, to protect owners' interests.

In the interests of completeness, it should be mentioned that transparent financial reporting rules, although necessary to make investment in Russia more attractive, is not sufficient. The Foreign Investment Advisory Council lists the following factors needed to attract international investment capital (ICAR Nov/Dec 2000):

- Accelerating the full transition to International Accounting Standards;
- Accelerating the adoption of PSA (Production Sharing Agreements) legislation and enabling regulations;
- Removing regional and interregional barriers restricting investment and business activities;
- Improving tax, customs and currency laws;
- Improving the banking system;
- Improving the protection of investors' rights, including the stock market; and
- Adding value to commercial activities of enterprises.

TRANSPARENCY OF FINANCIAL REPORTING

Below are the results of the research conducted by Troika Dialog (2001), the largest Russian investment company, which assessed the consistency of the most liquid shares for 28 listed Russian companies' corporate governance practices using World Economic Forum (WEF) principles. In aggregate, the market capitalization of these issuers totals $45 billion and represents around 85 percent of the total capitalization of the Russian market.

On the criterion "financial discipline," which was characterized by disclosure of accurate, consolidated, timely information using IFRS and verified by an independent audit, the 28 companies fared as follows:

Financial Discipline

Category	Number of Companies	Percent of Companies
Adequate to good	8	28
Fair to adequate	10	36
Poor to fair	<u>10</u>	<u>36</u>
Totals	28	100%

Thus, less than half of the companies in the sample adequately comply with the principles of financial discipline. However, the experts conducting the survey did remark that the trend is clearly improving. Another survey of 1040 accountants from average sized Russian companies found that 71 percent of the respondents did not think that financial statements adequately reflect the company's economic reality (Rozhnova 2000).

What is wrong with the financial information that Russian companies produce? Why do even the people who participate in creating the financial information think that the information quality of what they create is low? There are several reasons. To understand what Russian accounting represents, it is necessary to take a look at the recent past. The present state of Russian accounting can only be understood by looking at what went before and how it has evolved.

Soviet accounting played a dual role in the tight, centrally planned economy up until the last decade of the twentieth century (Enthoven 1992). First, it functioned to provide the country's top management with the information necessary to control the economy and meet the plan targets. Second, it was used as a mechanism to protect socialist property. The accountant's function was one of bookkeeping rather than what those in the West think of as accounting. Every step was prescribed by numerous and specific instructions. As a result, most of accounting consisted of filling out forms, mostly statistical in nature. The reports were summarized, but not consolidated, at each successively higher level of the hierarchy. So the State, in the person of its representatives at different levels, was the only user of accounting information.

The beginning of the 1990s was commemorated not only by privatization, the appearance of private property and private owners, but also by a revolution in Russia's tax system (Shleifer and Treisman 2000). Accounting data was used to determine the amount of taxes that companies should pay. The system of penalties for violations of the tax law stipulated that, for example, the failure to pay 100 rubles in tax would result in a 10,000 ruble penalty. A company's existence became dependent on the accuracy of accounting. The value of a qualified accountant, who was able to avoid problems with Russia's Internal Revenue Service, has increased incredibly. The prestige of the accounting profession has also increased considerably.

Since the start of conversion from central planning to a market economy, the business community increasingly regards the accounting function as a tool of communication with the tax authorities, and through them, with the State. This new way of looking at the role of accounting has been evolving in the mind of the business community for slightly more than ten years.

As a consequence, there have been changes in legislation, including tax legislation. Taxation and accounting are now legally separated from each other. As of 2003, only one tax, the real estate tax, is based on accounting rather than separate tax data. But even now most people consider Russia's Internal Revenue Service as the only user of accounting information. Furthermore, the Tax Code still stipulates punishment for breaking the accounting rules, even in cases where the violation does not affect the amount of taxes paid (Tax Code of Russian Federation, Prov. #120).

Some Russian companies have started to realize that the poor quality of their financial statements is making it more difficult to attract foreign capital. They find it difficult to borrow funds internationally or to place their stock on foreign stock exchanges. Their present financial statements do not meet the needs of investors, either current or potential. As a result, some Russian corporate executives have come to the realization that they must transform their financial statements, which are now prepared according to Russian Accounting Standards (RAS), into statements that satisfy IFRS requirements. However, in order to do that, Russian companies have to incur additional expenses. They have to prepare two sets of financial statements, those that comply with RAS and another set that complies with IFRS. They have to double the cost of audits, since one audit looks at RAS and another one must comply with International Standards on Auditing (ISA). The Troika Dialog research mentioned above found that, out of 34 companies having effective ADR programs, 8 converted their financial reports to comply with U.S. GAAP and 9 companies prepared financial statements in conformity with IFRS. In other words, only half of the companies examined prepared financial statements that followed some kind of internationally recognized financial statement principles (GAAP or IFRS).

At this point, one may ask the question: What is the essence of the fundamental differences between RAS and the standards used by developed market economies (GAAP or IFRS)? What is wrong with RAS that international investors of capital hesitate to place trust in RAS?

One reason why international investors hesitate to place much confidence in RAS is because of lack of familiarity. Investors feel much more comfortable reading financial statements that are prepared in accordance with a set of standards they are familiar with, whether those standards are U.S. GAAP or IFRS. But their lack of confidence in RAS cannot be blamed solely on lack of familiarity with RAS.

IFRS has a user orientation. Indeed, that is the basis of IFRS. In *Framework for the Preparation and Presentation of Financial Statements* (IASC 1989) it is stated that the objective of financial reporting is to prove information regarding an entity's financial position, performance, and changes in financial position to a broad spectrum of users to enable them to make rational and informed decisions (Epstein and Mirza 2003: 72).

IFRS set requirements and principles for financial reporting -- nature, measurement, presentation, substance over form, materiality, etc. Relying on these principles, accountants use their professional judgment to construct financial statements. The Russian system, on the other hand, is based on strictly regulated rules. Instructions, rather than professional judgment and principles, underlie accounting and financial reporting. When Western accountants encounter a situation that requires them to determine how a particular event should be recorded, they go to generally accepted accounting principles and exercise professional judgment to arrive at an answer. Russian accountants, at best, think about the instructions that might describe it. At worst, they pick up the telephone and call the auditor.

The Russian accounting environment has not yet adjusted to market-oriented accounting and the thought processes involved. They are not yet ready to accept the possibility that accountants can exercise professional judgment and can arrive at conclusions that result in financial statement figures that are not identical. Also, most accountants are not ready to make significant business decisions. One of the questions asked in the Rozhnova study (2000) that surveyed accountants at1040 companies was whether accounting rules should be detailed, prescribed and unambiguous. Fifty-eight percent of the accountants who answered that question said yes, indicating that the majority of Russian accountants are still hesitant to assume responsibility or exercise professional judgment. With this kind of mindset, it will take some time before Russian accountants are fully prepared to use Western, market oriented accounting systems, regardless of what the Russian legislature (Duma) says.

Even in the cases where the legislature offers a choice of different options, the first choice of many Russian accountants is to use the method that corresponds to the tax rules. Their second choice is to select the method that is least costly in terms of time and effort. Their last concern is how their choice will affect the financial statements.

One of the reasons why Russian accountants try to avoid expressing an opinion or making a decision regarding the preparation of financial statements is due to the Russian accounting mentality that has become ingrained over several generations of Soviet communist rule. Their thought process is rooted in the more than 70 year practice of "execution of commands from the top," coupled by a decade of recent experience of "walking over the precipice" with the threat of getting punished for making mistakes on a tax return.

Another factor that prevents the transformation from the "following instructions" approach to principles based accounting is the fact that none of the current regulations provide any concept of principle based accounting, the very concepts that underlie accounting systems in developed market economies. There are no definitions for assets, liabilities or capital in any Russian legislative act.

Coming back to the conceptual distinctions between IFRS and RAS it is necessary to stress the differences in disclosure. Despite the fact that Russian standards have made a big step forward in this respect -- today they require an amount of disclosure that was impossible to imagine not long ago (Shneydman 2002) -- it still is not good enough to provide sufficient transparency to satisfy most financial statement readers. Furthermore, in practice accountants often disdain disclosure requirements. For Russian accountants, notes do not play an important role as part of the financial statements. The reason is partly because of a lack of working experience where there is a possibility of having a choice or making a decision based on professional judgment. Another reason is because the main reader of financial statements, the Tax Service, pays almost no attention to footnotes. Despite all these reasons and factors, disclosure in Russian financial statements has improved greatly in recent years. Although the amount of disclosure given in Russian financial statements is still considered insufficient by market economy standards, the differences between Russian disclosure and disclosure in advanced market economies has narrowed considerably.

The beginning of the move toward heightened quality of financial statement disclosure was the adoption of the *Programme for the Reformation of Accounting in accordance with International Accounting Standards* in 1998. It was declared on the State (national) level that accounting systems should provide useful information to users, primarily investors. This document proposed that accounting reform should be focused toward the harmonisation of accounting standards at the international level and that methodological assistance should be rendered to enterprises in the comprehension and introduction of the reformed accounting model.

Of course the mere fact that such a program exists on paper does not mean that the task has been accomplished. In fact, the views of business owners toward the relevance and content of financial statements has changed very little since this Programme was launched.

More than five years have passed since 1998. What has been done? New terms that had not been used before in Russian accounting practice were introduced into accounting legislation. Examples include contingencies, segment information, materiality, discontinued operations, deferred tax assets and liabilities. New accounting standards based on IFRS were adopted. Most of them stipulate a scope of disclosure that is sufficient to consider the financial statements to be transparent.

The Cash Flow Statement and the Statement of Changes in Equity became a part of annual reports. The format of reporting is not mandatory but recommended. Enterprises are free to change it, following general reporting rules. Groups of companies (with subsidiaries) are supposed to prepare consolidated financial reports.

Another important point to mention is that IFRS have been translated into Russian. Readers who can read English might not appreciate this point, since they are accustomed to reading accounting rules, whether IFRS or U.S. GAAP, in their own language. Try to put yourself into the shoes of a Russian accountant. How would you, as an English speaker, like it if your government passed a law requiring you to construct your financial statements using Russian accounting rules if those rules were available only in Russian?

Translating IFRS into Russian was a big step forward, since it would be impossible to adopt and implement IFRS if no Russian version were available. However, problems remain, even with the Russian translation. The translation was made in 1999 and several important changes have been made since then. Russian translations have not kept up with these changes in the English version. Furthermore, the Russian translation contains some ambiguities and some substantive errors. For example, one of the important rules leaves out the word "not," leaving the Russian reader to believe that the rule says exactly the opposite of what it actually says.

Since IFRS have been translated into Russian they have become an obligatory part of the accounting curriculum at Russian universities. However, unlike in the West, there is not yet a strong secondary literature that provides explanations and examples of how the IFRS should be applied (Alexander and Archer; Epstein and Mirza). This problem will be solved in time, as Russian professors publish their class notes and write textbooks. Various Russian accounting associations are also creating literature that both students and professionals can refer to when they have questions about IFRS. The International Center for Accounting Reform [www.icar.ru] is one such organization.

Although Russia has more or less decided to move toward IFRS, it is unfair to characterize Russian accounting legislation as fully complying with IFRS requirements as of today. There is also a problem of sticking to IFRS once they have been adopted. There is evidence to suggest that banks tend to abandon IFRS when their operating results decline (Vysokov 2000). This countertrend does not help to improve the reliability of financial statements and tends to reduce the confidence international investors place in Russian financial statements.

Above we have attempted to describe the conceptual differences between the two systems. Below we will examine certain differences in the accounting for specific assets, liabilities, equity, income, expense and loss accounts. These differences can result in very different figures being reported in financial reports, since some important differences between RAS and IFRS have not yet been resolved.

It might also be pointed out that a company cannot state that its statements comply with IFRS unless they comply with *all* IFRS [IAS1.11, p. 16] Thus, any Russian company that follows IFRS to the extent possible, but either has not adopted all IFRS or has diverged here and there to comply with RAS where the two standards conflict cannot honestly say that it complies with IFRS. As a result, an honest Russian company cannot announce to the international capital market that its financial reports follow IFRS even in cases where such rules are followed completely, except for minor inconsequential exceptions.

Much of the information used in this section below was taken from *GAAP 2000: A Survey of National Accounting Rules in 53 Countries* (Andersen et al 2000) supplemented by more recent data (Arthur Andersen et al 2001; BDO et al 2002). One area of difference that authors frequently examine is the difference between RAS and IFRS in the area of allocating administrative overhead costs (Ramcharran 2000; Enthoven 1999). Experts point out that the Russian accounting system uses a different approach than that used in the West. Russian legislation allows companies to spread these costs among the various categories of inventory, whereas Western rules require companies to treat these costs as period costs and deduct them at the end of the period. As a result, profits are overestimated in one period and underestimated in another period. The cost of renting production facilities is not included in the cost of production, either, which distorts profits and profitability ratios. (Ramcharran 2000). An alternative method that recognizes period costs as incurred has been permitted since 1991 but has not been widely practiced, mostly because companies generally structure their accounting rules to parallel the tax rules. Russian accounting systems tend to be tax driven. Tax rules do not permit a company to decrease taxable income by including overhead costs at the time they occur.

Another major difference between RAS and IFRS is that RAS allow a kind of fund accounting system for liabilities that permits Russian companies to set up reserves against expenses and losses (Enthoven 1999). This practice can result in distorting income, since expenses that were incurred in one year may be deducted in another year. Also, the Russian accounting mentality has not yet erased the old methods from their memory banks and accounting practices. Before 1992, the only acceptable accounting method in Russia was the cash method. However, although it is now possible to use the accrual method, the cash method still dominates. Another difference between RAS and IFRS is that RAS classify bonds under equity, whereas they are classified as liabilities under IFRS. (Ramcharran 2000).

Sometimes it is possible to reconcile these differences. The problem is that doing so is burdensome and time consuming. It is also not always possible to convert RAS to IFRS because financial analysts do not have sufficient information to perform the calculations. If the goal of financial reporting is to attract foreign direct investment, Russian companies that do not follow IFRS are placing themselves at a competitive disadvantage. Why should financial analysts have to take the time and trouble to convert RAS to IFRS when they can look at the financial statements of any number of non-Russian firms without having to make any conversion calculations?

Another problem with RAS is the lack of guidance on how to deal with inflation. The result is often misleading or distorted financial statements. According to IAS 29, one hyperinflationary sign is a cumulative inflation rate over three years approaching 100 percent. Taking into account that, for 1991-2001, prices rose by about 92 percent, according to State Statistic Committee data, financial statement figures would be subject to correction.

At the time this paper is being written (May 2003) there are no rules regulating the following items according to RAS:

- the classification of business combinations between acquisitions and unitings of interest (IAS 22.8),
- provisions in the context of business combinations accounted for as acquisitions (IAS 22.31),
- the translation of the financial statements of hyperinflationary subsidiaries (IAS 21.36),
- the recognition of operating lease incentives (IAS 17.2; SIC 15),
- accounting for defined benefit pension plans and some other types of employee benefits (IAS 19.52),
- the treatment of exchange differences resulting from severe devaluation or depreciation of a currency (IAS 21.21; SIC 11),
- the notion and definition of cash equivalents (IAS 7.6),
- detailed guidance on preparation of cash flow statements (IAS 7),
- consolidation of special purpose entities (SIC 12).

In RAS there are no specific rules requiring disclosure of:

- a primary statement of changes in equity (IAS 1.7) and a primary statement of cash flows (IAS 7),
- the FIFO or current cost of inventories valued on the LIFO basis (IAS 2.36).

Other differences concern the valuation of goodwill; methods of fundamental error correction; non-monetary transaction revenue recognition rules; lessors' income recognition; provisions recognition; conditions and rules of preparing consolidated reports, etc.

Since the large accounting firm reports of 2000 and 2001 (Arthur Andersen et al 2000; Andersen et al 2001) many differences have been eliminated. Impairment of assets, regulated by IAS 36, is stipulated by PBU 5/01. Accounting for deferred tax, regulated by IAS 12, has been introduced by PBU 18/02 for financial reporting starting in 2003. With the adoption of PBU 19/02, "Accounting for Investment Activity," most differences concerning accounting for financial instruments have been overcome. PBU 16/02 includes provisions for discontinued operations and related disclosures (IAS 35). Distinctions between principles of the determination period of depreciation of property, plant and equipment (IAS 16) are eliminated by PBU 3-6/01.

As a result of the recent adoption of these additional accounting rules, Russian accounting rules are moving closer to IFRS in terms of reliability and transparency of financial reporting information. Financial reports prepared in accordance with RAS are getting closer to reports prepared on the basis of IFRS. This convergence allowed one of Russia's Finance Ministers (Shatalov 2003) to say that, whereas a few years ago if a Russian company or bank could make a profit of 100 according to RAS and, at the same time lose 20 according to IFRS, today this proportion is about 100-85.

As can be seen, Russian accounting regulation cannot be said to be in full compliance with IFRS. However, there are several opinions regarding where to go from here. Some experts, including Ministry of Finance authorities, are inclined to favor a gradualist approach. RAS should move toward IFRS bit by bit. Supporters of this position reasonably argue that accounting is a component part of the national environment, including the economy, culture, history, etc. Accounting development cannot pass ahead of other parts of the economy. For example, the problems with fair value implementation cannot be solved in one hour because the market in Russia is not sufficiently developed, especially the stock market. The disadvantage of following this gradualist approach is that Russia's planned regulatory changes will trail behind the changes made to IFRS.

Another approach might be labeled the shock approach. This approach involves adopting all IFRS in a single day. One advantage of this approach is that it would bring to an end the constant changes that Russian accountants have had to deal with for the last decade. One potential problem with this approach is that instantaneous adoption of IFRS might not be followed by support in implementation. It is one thing to change an entire set of rules and quite another to have the accounting profession snap to attention to implement them, especially when many members of the accounting profession are not familiar with the new rules or with some of the more sophisticated aspects of a market economy.

The second approach -- shock treatment -- seems to be the more efficient option. But this approach can be successful only if the transition to IFRS is comprehensively prepared. Methodological manuals, explanations and practical examples must be developed and clarified for accountants *before* the date when the new Standards go into effect, not after. Current legislation should be adjusted to the new rules. As for insufficient development of present market instruments in Russia's economy, the delay of introducing advanced market oriented accounting rules might serve to impede their evolution. Preparing the way by having the rules in place could serve to facilitate the transition to a modern economy. Failure to have market oriented financial reporting rules in place could lead to a Catch-22 situation, where the old rules impede economic progress and lack of economic progress vitiate the need for new and better rules.

It is believed that the creation of legislative base is a guarantee of successful reform, including accounting reform. But, to draft and adopt a new law or regulation is not sufficient. Passage does not guarantee that the new law will work in practice. Financial reports that comply with IFRS will come into existence only if the accountants who prepare the reports follow the rules of financial reporting. Otherwise, the beauty, elegance and rigor of the rules will be useless. For accountants to execute all requirements properly, it is necessary to:
   • be knowledgeable and to understand them,
   • be qualified to apply them, and
   • be willing to follow them.

There is a very real possibility that, to solve this problem of what may be called the human factor, the solution to this aspect of the problem may be more difficult than to change legislation. There are several reasons for this difficulty. We have attempted to examine some of them above. There is the perception that tax officials are the main users of financial reporting information. That is, by the way, the reason why many provisions of the new standards are just ignored by accountants. There is a tendency to think that "if the tax inspector doesn't need it, I don't, either." Accountants just don't take notice of some new rules.

Other human problems exist as well. An accountant's mentality is one of them. Accountants are not accustomed to making decisions. In the old days they didn't have to. They just followed the rules. They have difficulty understanding the new standards in the absence of manuals. They are just plain tired of the constant changes that have been made to the accounting and tax rules since the introduction of the market economy. A similar thing happened to accountants during the 1980s, when Congress was passing major tax reform legislation practically every year and the Financial Accounting Standards Board was issuing numerous complicated financial reporting rules. The terms used to describe this phenomenon and the effect it had was accounting standard overload. Russian accountants have been experiencing the same thing.

Another factor to consider is that, in order to succeed with the implementation of any policy is that there must be support at the micro level. Company accountants must support the changes if they are to be implemented effectively. And last but not least, there must be demand for quality financial information.

RUSSIA'S COMPETITIVE POSITION FOR FOREIGN DIRECT INVESTMENT

A survey conducted by the large accounting firms found that more than 90 percent of the world's major economies plan to adopt or converge with IFRS (BDO et al 2002). That being the case, it becomes imperative that Russia adopt IFRS in order to compete for international capital. Doing that will be problem enough, as we have pointed out. However, that is not the only problem that Russia must solve to be internationally competitive for foreign direct investment. Russia must compete with more than 100 other countries for foreign capital.

For each of the past few years the Heritage Foundation and the Wall Street Journal have published a study that measures economic freedom for more than 150 countries, which are ranked based on the scores they receive in a number of areas. A score of 1.0 is best; 5.0 is worst. Their *2003 Index of Economic Freedom* ranks Hong Kong as the world's most free economy with an overall score of 1.45. Russia's overall rank was 135 out of 161 countries with an overall score of 3.70. What this ranking means is that, all other things being equal, there are 134 countries that investors would probably find more attractive for investment purposes than Russia, if one begins with the premise that investing in a free economy is more attractive than investing in an economy that is not free. That is bad news for the Russian economy, which needs massive injections of foreign capital in order to grow.

Table 1
Overall Ranking in Terms of Economic Freedom
Russia Compared to other Former Soviet Countries

Former Soviet Country	Rank (out of 161 countries)	Score 1 to 5, where 1 is best
Estonia	6	1.80
Lithuania	29	2.35
Latvia	33	2.45
Armenia	44	2.65
Moldova	92	3.20
Azerbaijan	104	3.35
Kyrgyz Republic	104	3.35
Georgia	113	3.40
Kazakhstan	119	3.50

Ukraine	131	3.65
Russia	**135**	**3.70**
Tajikistan	143	3.95
Turkmenistan	146	4.15
Uzbekistan	149	4.25
Belarus	151	4.30

Source: Heritage Foundation and Wall Street Journal, *2003 Index of Economic Freedom*
[www.heritage.org]

Table 1 shows Russia's overall ranking compared to other former Soviet republics. Ten of the 15 former Soviet republics had higher overall scores than Russia, with Estonia, Lithuania, Latvia and Armenia doing quite well by world standards. Only four former Soviet republics had lower overall rankings than Russia. That is bad news for Russian companies that are seeking foreign capital because this statistics shows that Russia is not a very desirable place to invest. More than half of the former Soviet republics are better overall, in terms of economic freedom.

One set of factors in the Heritage study measures the freedom to invest. To receive a good score in this category, countries must maintain liberal policies regarding capital flows and investment. Their foreign investment code must be transparent and open. Foreign investments must be treated impartially and there must be an efficient approval process. Any restrictions on foreign investment must be few and economically insignificant.

Measuring Russia's ranking in this category (freedom to invest) involves some calculations and value judgment. Russia's score was 3.0. Fifty-two countries had higher scores. Twelve received a score of 1.0 and forty had scores of 2.0. Seventy-five countries received scores of 3.0. So Russia is tied with 74 other countries. Twenty-four countries received scores of 4.0, five countries had scores of 5.0 and five countries were unranked in this category. If one had to pick a number to rank each country included in the study, it might be reasonable to rank as #6 all those countries that had a score of 1.0, since 12 countries had this score and 6 is about the midpoint. If we use this methodology to rank countries in terms of desirability for foreign investment, then the 40 countries that had a score of 2.0 would each be ranked 32 [12 + 0.5(40)], and the 75 countries receiving a score of 3.0 would be ranked 89 [52 + 0.5(75)]. The 24 countries that had a score of 4.0 would each be ranked 139 [127 + 0.5(24)] and the five countries with scores of 5.0 would be ranked 154 [151 + 0.5(5)]. Table 2 shows where Russia stands in the rankings compared to the other former Soviet countries. Table 3 shows the number of countries in each of the five categories.

Table 2
Ranking in Terms of Foreign Investment
Russia Compared to other Former Soviet Countries

Former Soviet Country	Rank (out of 161 countries)	Score 1 to 5, where 1 is best
Estonia	6	1.0
Lithuania	32	2.0
Latvia	32	2.0
Armenia	32	2.0
Moldova	89	3.0
Kyrgyz Republic	89	3.0
Georgia	89	3.0
Russia	**89**	**3.0**
Azerbaijan	139	4.0
Kazakhstan	139	4.0
Ukraine	139	4.0
Tajikistan	139	4.0
Turkmenistan	139	4.0
Uzbekistan	139	4.0
Belarus	139	4.0

Source: Heritage Foundation and Wall Street Journal, *2003 Index of Economic Freedom*
[www.heritage.org]

Table 3
Foreign Investment
Frequency Distribution

Score	Number of Countries	Cumulative	Rank
1.0	12	12	6
2.0	40	52	32
3.0	75	127	89
4.0	24	151	139
5.0	5	156	154
unranked	5	161	

As can be seen in Table 2, four of the 15 former Soviet republics ranked higher than Russia and 7 ranked lower. Three other former republics were in the same category as Russia. Estonia was the only former Soviet republic to earn a score of 1.0. Latvia, Lithuania and Armenia had scores of 2.0. None of the republics had a score of 5.0.

CONCLUDING COMMENTS

Based on the statistics in the Heritage study, combined with the fact that Russia has not yet fully adopted accounting standards that international investors trust, one might conclude that nobody wants to invest in Russia. Luckily, such is not the case. Billions of dollars are pouring into the Russian economy for some reason, in spite of the fact that there are many more desirable places to invest and despite the fact that the integrity of Russian financial reports often leaves much to be desired. Exploring the reasons for this foreign investment would take us beyond the scope of this paper.

What this paper shows is that financial transparency is desirable if the goal is to attract foreign investment, that financial transparency is difficult to achieve in a country where accountants are not accustomed to disclosing financial information and that Russia is making progress in adopting and implementing accounting standards that are internationally recognized and trusted. However, Russia has a long way to go before the financial statements its companies publish are considered as trustworthy as the statements issued by more mature market economies. Russia must complete the IFRS adoption process, educate accountants and auditors about their importance as well has their technical aspects and implement them throughout the economy. A good start has been made but it will be a few years before the goal is reached.

REFERENCES

Alexander, David and Simon Archer. 2003. *Miller International Accounting Standards Guide.* New York: Aspen Law & Business.

Andersen, BDO, Deloitte Touche Tohmatsu, Ernst & Young, Grant Thornton, KPMG and PricewaterhouseCoopers. *GAAP 2001: A Survey of National Accounting Rules Benchmarked against International Accounting Standards.* The Russian Federation is covered at pp. 110-113. Available at [www.pwcglobal.com]

Arndt, H.W. 1987. *Economic Development: The History of an Idea.* Chicago: University of Chicago Press.

Arthur Andersen, BDO, Deloitte Touche Tohmatsu, Ernst & Young International, Grant Thornton, KPMG and PricewaterhouseCoopers. *GAAP 2000: A Survey of National Accounting Rules in 53 Countries.* The Russian Federation is covered at pp. 89-91. Available at [www.pwcglobal.com]

Bauer, Peter. 1991. *The Development Frontier: Essays in Applied Economics.* Cambridge, MA: Harvard University Press.

Bauer, Peter. 1976. *Dissent on Development*, revised edition. Cambridge, MA: Harvard University Press.

BDO, Deloitte Touche Tohmatsu, Ernst & Young, Grant Thornton, KPMG and PricewaterhouseCoopers. *GAAP Convergence 2002: A Survey of National Efforts to Promote and Achieve Convergence with International Financial Reporting Standards*. Available at [www.pwcglobal.com]

Damant, David. 1999. IASs and the Capital Markets. *Accountancy: International Edition*, Vol. 123, No. 1269 (May), p. 80.

Enthoven, Adolf J.H. 1992. Accounting in Russia: From Perestroika to Profits. *Management Accounting* (October), 27-31.

Epstein, Barry J. and Abbas Ali Mirza. 2003. *IAS 2003: Interpretation and Application of International Accounting Standards*. New York: John Wiley & Sons.

Hanke, Steve H. and Alan A. Walters, editors. 1991. *Capital Markets and Development*. San Francisco: ICS Press.

Heritage Foundation and Wall Street Journal. 2002. *2003 Index of Economic Freedom* [www.heritage.org/research/features/index/2003/index.html]

IASC (International Accounting Standards Committee). 1989. *Framework for the Preparation and Presentation of Financial Statements*. London: IASC.

ICAR (International Center for Accounting Reform). 2001. Recommendations for Accounting Reform in the CIS Countries. *ICAR Newsletter*, May/June. [www.icar.ru/eng/newsletter/22/6/2001.html]

ICAR. 2001a. Poor Compliance and Poor Auditing Undermines Achievements on International Accounting Standards. *ICAR Newsletter*, March/April [www.icar.ru/eng/newsletter/4.4.2001.html]

ICAR. 2001b. EU Takes Important Step in Support of Russia's Auditing Reform. *International Center for Accounting Reform Newsletter* March/April. [www.icar.ru/eng/newsletter/15.4.2001.html]

ICAR. 2000. Communique of the Thirteenth Session of the Foreign Investment Advisory Council in Russia. *International Center for Accounting Reform Newsletter*. November/December. [www.icar.ru/eng/newsletter/2.12.2000.html]

ICAR. 2000a. ERBD Calls for Use of IAS. *International Center for Accounting Reform Newsletter,* November/December. [www.icar.ru/eng/newsletter/4.12.2000.html]

Lal, Deepak. 2001. *Unintended Consequences: The Impact of Factor Endowments, Culture and Politics on Long-Term Economic Performance*. Cambridge, MA: MIT Press.

Lal, Deepak. 1986. *The Poverty of Development Economics*. Cambridge, MA: Harvard University Press.

Larson, Robert K. and Sara York. 1996. Accounting Standard-Setting Strategies and Theories of Economic Development: Implications for the Adoption of International Accounting Standards. *Advances in International Accounting,* Vol. 9, pp. 1-20.

Larson, Robert K. 1993. International Accounting Standards and Economic Growth: An Empirical Investigation of Their Relationship in Africa. *Research in Third World Accounting*, Vol. 2, pp. 27-43.

Radoutsky, Alexander. 2001. Transparent Financial Information as a Factor of Economic Stability and Intensive Growth. *International Center for Accounting Reform Newsletter*, March/April. [www.icar.ru/eng/newsletter/17.4.2001.html]

Ramcharran, Harri. 2000. The Need for International Accounting Harmonization: An Examination and Comparison of the Practices of Russian Banks. *American Business Review* 18:1 (January): 1-8.

Rozhnova, Olga. 2000. The Problem of Perception of the New Russian Accounting Standards. *International Center for Accounting Reform Newsletter,* November/December [www.icar.ru/eng/newsletter/13.12.2000.html]

Russian Federation. 1998. Programme for the Reformation of Accounting in Accordance with IAS. Decision of Government of Russian Federation #283, March 6.

Shatalov, S. 2003. Russian Standards Approach IFRS. *Prime-TASS*. Business type. 01.23.03.

Shleifer, Andrei and Daniel Treisman. 2000. Without a Map: Political Tactics and Economic Reform in Russia. Cambridge and London: The MIT Press.

Shneydman, L. 2002. Introduction of IAS in Russia. *ICAR Newsletter*, April 1 [www.icar.ru/rus/newsletter/1/4/2002]

Tax Code of the Russian Federation, Provision #120.

Troika Dialog. 2001. *Corporate Governance Principles*. Review for WEF. [www.troika.ru]

Vorushkin, Vladimir. 2001. IAS Benefits for Russian Enterprises: Managerial Issues. *International Center for Accounting Reform Newsletter*, March/April. [www.icar.ru/eng/newsletter/19.4.2001.html]

Vysokov, V. 2000. Center-invest: Banking in Russia using International Accounting Standards. *Euromoney*, Issue 377 (September), 117.

Chapter 6

TAXATION AND PUBLIC FINANCE IN RUSSIA[*]

Abstract

Countries that are moving from central planning to a market economy face unique problems in many areas, including taxation and public finance. The methods of collecting the revenue needed to fund government services were much different under a socialist system. Shifting to a market system requires government to create new institutions and methods of collecting revenue. All transition economies face similar problems in this regard and several different approaches have been tried in an attempt to find the solution that is best for each particular country. This paper summarizes the methods the Russian Federation is using and comments on the problems Russia still faces as it attempts to install a system of taxation and public finance that is appropriate for its emerging market economy.

INTRODUCTION

Collecting revenue needed to pay for state functions was relatively easy under the old Soviet regime. The government owned everything and it was able to collect from its various production units. In the old days more than 90 percent of state budget revenues were collected from state enterprises (Easter 2002: n.9, citing Tolkushkin, 2001). The turnover tax and the profits tax on state enterprises were the two main sources of revenue. During the later stages of the Soviet regime the amount of revenue extracted from state enterprise profit taxes declined, so much so that the Soviet government had to increase the turnover tax to compensate for the shortfall in enterprise taxes. When that strategy failed, the government resorted to borrowing to pay government expenses, which led to an inflationary spiral (Easter 2003).

This whole system changed when Russia started shifting away from a centrally planned economy and toward a decentralized market economy. A

---

[*] An earlier version of this chapter was presented at the 16th Annual Conference of the International Academy of Business Disciplines, San Antonio, March 25-28, 2004

whole new infrastructure had to be built from scratch and developed into an efficient tax collecting machine. The present Russian system started its evolutionary (or revolutionary) process in 1991, when the first tax reforms were introduced. Tax reforms continue to be introduced. In fact, so many tax reform initiatives and suggestions have been introduced in recent years that it has caused a degree on instability. Taxpayers and investors like to know what the rules of the game are, and they do not like the rules to change often (McGee 2004). Thus, introducing frequent changes into the system destabilizes it. That is what happened in Russia in the early stages of the conversion process from a centrally planned economy to a market economy. As the Russian tax system matures and evolves it is expected that the rate or frequency of change will decline. That will be good news for investors and businesses, since the degree of instability and uncertainty will be reduced.

In the early days, four distinct philosophical groups emerged within the Russian government and in the private sector. They all wanted to influence tax policy and they wanted to influence it in different ways. Similar groups or factions exist in developed market economies as well, to varying degrees.

One group took a liberal market position. They wanted the tax system to stimulate economic growth. A second group, representing the interests of the post-communist industrial and financial elite, wanted the tax system to actively promote industrial development. They differed from the first group, in that they were interventionist in their thinking, whereas the first group favored a more hands-off policy.

The third group could be labeled fiscal federalists. They represented the interests of the regions and viewed the tax system as a means to increase regional political autonomy and power. The fourth group could be labeled fiscal populists. This group consisted mostly of left-wing political parties that had their base in the legislature. They viewed tax policy as a tool for redistribution of wealth and advocated high tax rates for the large existing corporations as well as on the emerging private sector (Easter 2003). Enthoven et al. (1998) state that the first group, the liberals, the group that favors economic growth, has the upper hand, although they also say that the growth policy advocated by the liberals would allow Russia to begin an industrial policy program, which better describes the second group.

None of these approaches to tax policy are new. They have all been discussed extensively in the literature by numerous authors over the years, including Bird (1992), Breton (1998), Buchanan (1967), Buchanan and Flowers (1975), Cullis and Jones (1998), McGee (2004, 1993) and Musgrave (1976, 1959).

In late 1991, the Russian government began its shock program of tax reform. It more or less modeled its new tax system after the advanced tax systems of the developed economies. It scrapped its turnover tax and replaced it with a value added tax (VAT). It instituted excise taxes on business and income taxes on individuals while retaining the profits tax on enterprises (Easter 2003).

TAX RATES

Tax rates in Russia change so frequently that it is difficult to keep up to date. The Russian government knows this, and is trying to address this issue by having less frequent changes. The tax rates below are based on the most current information the authors were able to find and were taken from several sources (KPMG 2003; PricewaterhouseCoopers, n.d.; Ernst & Young, 2002).

Tax Rates in Russia

Profits Tax	24% maximum (was 35%)
VAT	18% (2004); 20% (2003). A 10% rate applies to certain items such as books, periodicals, medical goods, children's clothes and food.
Unified Social (Payroll) Tax	Regressive scale from 35.6% down to 2% assessed to the employer. Assessed for the Pension Fund, the Social Insurance Fund and the Medical Insurance Fund.
Individual Income Tax	13% flat tax for residents; 30% for non-residents.
Import Duties	20-30%
Property Tax	Assessed by regions on tangibles, intangibles, inventory and prepaid expenses. . Cannot exceed 2% of the taxable base.
Sales Tax	Local tax, not to exceed 5%.
Tax on use of words "Russia," "Russian Federation"	Russian firms that use these words or derivatives of these words as part of their names generally pay a tax equal to 0.5% of gross sales.

The tendency in the past has been to look at the form of a transaction rather than the substance, which has led to a great deal of tax abuse (or planning opportunities, depending on whether you are a tax official or a taxpayer). The trend is now shifting more toward substance rather than form (PricewaterhouseCoopers, n.d.).

It is surprising to many commentators that Russia and several other former Soviet republics and East European countries have adopted a flat tax, since the United States has been trying to adopt such a tax for several decades, so far unsuccessfully. Alvin Rabushka, one of the leading advocates of the flat tax in the United States (Rabushka and Ryan, 1982; Hall and Rabushka, 1985), has written several articles praising this Russian move, and hoping that the United States will finally catch on and adopt the Russian tax system (Rabushka, 2002a, b, c). Steve Forbes (2003) points out that Russia, Estonia, Latvia, Slovakia and Ukraine have adopted the flat tax, and says it is about time the United States does so, too. Advocates of the flat tax see it as eliminating much of the complication of the present tax code while creating incentives that spur economic growth. Opponents of the flat tax concept want a progressive system that would place a heavier burden on the rich, who supposedly have more ability to pay (McCaffery 2002). Opponents of the ability to pay concept see soak the rich schemes as a negative sum game from the utilitarian perspective (Blum and Kalven, 1953) as well as an unfair punishment for the most productive people in society (de Jouvenel 1952, 1990).

COLLECTION

Changing from a centrally planned system, where the government owns everything, to a market economy, where power and economic resources are dispersed, creates transition problems in many areas, and collecting tax revenue is one of them. There was basically no infrastructure in place to deal with revenue collection in the private sector because there was no private sector, so a collection mechanism had to be put in place, tweaked as the finance ministry moved down the learning curve and refined as conditions changed. One especially interesting change involved the attempt to computerize the tax system and use bar codes to make tax returns machine readable. Such an idea seems perfectly reasonable to a technocrat or bureaucrat and was not expected to meet with any opposition. But such was not the case.

Portions of the Russian Orthodox Church objected. A large segment of the Russian population (as well as the populations of many other countries) regards the national tax collection agency as a kind of Antichrist to begin with. But trying to incorporate bar codes into the tax collection system was too much for some Russian Orthodox members to take.

Their opposition stems from the Bible's Book of Revelations, which states that, as the end of the world draws near, "the Beast" will force people to have a mark placed on their foreheads and right hands. Those who do not have the beast's mark will not be able to buy or sell. The Beast's number in the Book of Revelations is 666, which is similar to the stripes of binary code at the beginning, middle and end of bar codes (Anon. 2001a). This similarity has been noticed by Christian fundamentalists in the United States as well, who are actively attacking the U.S. government's proposal to implant a binary chip into the bodies of U.S. citizens as a means of controlling illegal immigration.

The furor against this proposal died down somewhat when leaders of the Russian Orthodox Church established a theological commission to look into the matter. The commission found no basis in the allegation that the use of bar codes would bring about the end of the world any sooner or even that all bar codes contain the binary code for 666. The theological commission issued a seven-page document asking employers to be understanding if some employees declined the tax numbers they were assigned. It also firmly rebuked the zealots who were pushing the idea that everyone must reject the bar code assigned to them lest they risk eternal damnation.

The Russian tax police are not known for their compassion or willingness to listen to a taxpayer's problems. They are often viewed as evil because of their mafia-like collection methods, which at times involve machine guns, baseball bats and ski masks (Anon. 2001a). A number of Russian tax collectors have been killed in the line of duty. Bribery and corruption are rampant.

The founders of Russia's tax police include a major general and eleven colonels from the KGB and eight colonels from the MVD. Mid-level employees include more than a thousand KGB and MVD officers and 3490 Ministry of Defense officers (Easter 2002:n. 87). Thus there is the perception as well as the reality that the tax police are a tough bunch.

There is the widespread perception among taxpayers in Russian speaking countries that they do not owe the government anything because the government doesn't do anything for them. Or because it does more to them than for them (McGee, 1999). Nearly half of the taxes owed in Russia never get paid (Anon. 1998a).

Boris Yeltsin launched a television ad campaign to persuade the public that they had a civic duty to pay their taxes. Some of the ads took the form of cartoons that targeted the children of tax delinquents. Other ads were launched to inform the Russian public that assets confiscated by the tax authorities could be purchased in an old warehouse the tax police has set up at very low prices. The ads were made as much to educate (and terrify) Russian taxpayers as to raise revenue from the sale of the confiscated assets. Some of the ads also appealed to guilt by showing scenes of pensioners who could not be paid because the government could not collect the taxes to pay them. The International Monetary Fund has withheld payment on several loans it made to the Russian government because of its inability to collect taxes (Myre 1996).

In 1998, tax chief Boris Fyodorov announced that he would target Russia's rich and famous. The move was aimed not so much at collecting taxes from these targets as to send a message to all Russians who consider evading taxes. He targeted the rich and famous because of the publicity he would get. Only 4 million of Russia's 150 million population paid income taxes in 1997 and this policy of going after high profile individuals was expected to encourage ordinary Russians to start paying taxes. Some commentators doubted that the policy would have its intended effect, since tax evasion is burned so deeply into the Russian psyche. One tax specialist pointed out that the richest people in Russia are in the government and suggested that the tax police go after top government officials first (Baker 1998).

Targeting the rich and famous carries with it some negative externalities. When the tax police arrested Mikhail Khodorkovsky, Russia's richest man and chief of Yukos, Russia's largest oil company, it was thought that his arrest would send chills through the Russian stock market, causing it to plunge, and sending negative messages to foreign investors, who would be more hesitant to risk their assets by investing in Russia. His arrest was thought to be politically motivated. He had been giving financial support to several opposition political parties that were structuring themselves to challenge President Putin during the next election. At least one commentator has referred to his arrest as a political contract hit (Anon. 2003a).

Another part of the problem with collection stems from the fact that Russian tax laws are often deliberately unclear (Akhitirov 2003). There is ample opportunity to interpret the law in such a way that minimizes tax liability. There are also a number of political reasons for constraining collection efforts (Easter 2002).

TAX REFORM

Numerous proposals have been made for tax reform. Shleifer and Treisman (2000) point out that overgrazing of overlapping tax bases, tax sharing, divided control over tax collectors and confiscatory tax rates all combined to provide disincentives for paying taxes. They recommend that one way of reducing tax collection problems would be to separate the tax bases assigned to the various levels of government to the extent possible and separate the tax collection agencies. Separating tax bases could be achieved by assigning all revenues collected from the VAT to government X and all corporate income tax collected to government Y.

Another part of their tax reform plan would be to have separate tax collection agencies at the local, regional and national levels of government. Regional governments would assess rates and do the collections for the corporate profits tax and the corporate property tax within their region and get to keep whatever they collected. For corporations that were in more than one region, the proceeds would be dividing between or among the regions affected. The federal government would collect and keep all revenues from the VAT, excise taxes and taxes raised by international trade. Federal law would define tax bases so they do not overlap.

Their proposal would divide responsibility for the various taxes as follows:

Allocation of the Tax Function

	Rate Set by	Revenue Owned by
Export and import duties	Federal	Federal
VAT	Federal	Federal
Excises	Federal	Federal
Corporate profit tax	Regional	Regional
Corporate property tax	Regional	Regional
Tax on natural resources	Federal law	Regional
Taxes on small firms	Local	Local
Personal income tax	Local	Local
Personal property tax	Local	Local

Source: Shleifer & Treisman (2000): 158.

Adopting this approach would reduce the aggregate tax burden, which results when overlapping political jurisdictions tap into the same tax base. Federal government revenue would rise because the VAT is easier to collect than the income tax.

CONCLUDING COMMENTS

Russia has been going through rapid systemic economic changes for more than a decade. One of the major structural changes has been the shift of its system of public finance to accommodate its emerging market economy. The transition is far from complete. Russia's tax authorities still have a difficult time raising the revenue they need to provide government services. However, as the system becomes more stable and less complex and as tax rates continue to decline, economic growth will follow, or at least that is what the liberal economists predict. It will be interesting to see how Russia's system of public finance evolves over the next few years and whether the economists' prediction of economic growth is accurate.

REFERENCES

Akhitirov, Artyam. 2003. Does Anyone Pay Taxes These Days? *Pravda.Ru.* November 19. http://english.pravda.ru/printed.html?news_id=11303.

Anon. 2003a. Russia's Richest Man Arrested on Fraud, Tax Evasion Charges. *Yahoo! News Asia.* October 26. http://asia.news.yahoo.com/031025/afp/031025201623eco.html.

Anon. 2001a. Finance and Economics: Tax Beast. *The Economist* 358(8211): 71 (March 3).

Anon. 1998a. Russia's Tax Revulsion. *The Christian Science Monitor*, March 12.

Baker, Stephanie. 1998. Russia: Tax Chief Targets Rich and Famous. *Radio Free Europe*, Radio Liberty, June 5. www.rferl.org/nca/features/1998/06/F.RU.98060152350.html.

Bird, Richard M. 1992. *Tax Policy & Economic Development*. Baltimore and London: The Johns Hopkins University Press.

Blum, Walter J. and Harry Kalven, Jr. 1953. *The Uneasy Case for Progressive Taxation*. Chicago: University of Chicago Press.

Breton, Albert. 1998. *Competitive Governments: An Economic Theory of Politics and Public Finance*. Cambridge, UK and New York: Cambridge University Press.

Buchanan, James M. 1967. *Public Finance in Democratic Process*. Chapel Hill: University of North Carolina Press.

Buchanan, James M. and Marilyn R. Flowers. 1975. *The Public Finances*, 4th edition. Homewood, IL: Richard D. Irwin, Inc.

Cullis, John and Philip Jones. 1998. *Public Finance and Public Choice*. New York: Oxford University Press.

De Jouvenel, Bertrand. 1952; 1990. *The Ethics of Redistribution*. Cambridge, UK: Cambridge University Press (1952); Indianapolis: Liberty Press, 1990).

Easter, Gerald M. 2003. Building State Capacity in Post-Communist Russia: Tax Collection. www.ilpp.ru/projects/govern/pdf/Easter_full.pdf.

Easter, Gerald M. 2002. Politics of Revenue Extraction in Post-Communist States: Poland and Russia Compared. *Politics & Society* 30(4): 599-627.

Enthoven, Adolf, Yaroslav V. Sokolov, Svetlana M. Bychkova, Valery V. Kovalev and Maria V. Semenova. 1998. *Accounting, Auditing and Taxation in the Russian Federation*. A joint publication of the IMA Foundation for Applied Research, Montvale, New Jersey and The Center for International Accounting Development, University of Texas at Dallas.

Ernst & Young. 2002. *Tax Tables 2003 Russia*. www.ey.com.

Forbes, Steve. 2003. Where Communists Beat Capitalists. *Forbes* 172(2): 16, July 21.

Hall, Robert E. and Alvin Rabushka. 1985. *The Flat Tax*. Stanford: Hoover Institution Press.

KPMG. 2003. *Doing Business in Russia* (July).

McCaffery, Edward J. 2002. *Fair Not Flat: How to Make the Tax System Better and Simpler*. Chicago: University of Chicago Press.

McGee, Robert W. 2004. *The Philosophy of Taxation and Public Finance*. Dordrecht, London and Boston: Kluwer Academic Publishers.

McGee, Robert W. 1999. Why People Evade Taxes in Armenia: A Look at an Ethical Issue Based on a Summary of Interviews. *Journal of Accounting, Ethics & Public Policy* 2(2): 408-416.

McGee, Robert W. 1993. Principles of Taxation for Emerging Economies: Lessons from the U.S. Experience. *Dickinson Journal of International Law* 12: 29-93.

Musgrave, Richard A. 1959. *The Theory of Public Finance: A Study in Public Economy.* New York, London and Toronto: McGraw-Hill Book Company.

Musgrave, Richard A. and Peggy B. Musgrave. 1976. *Public Finance in Theory and Practice*, 2nd edition. New York: McGraw-Hill Book Company.

Myre, Greg. 1996. In Russia, Tax Police Take New Approach to Cash Crisis. *Associated Press*, December 6.
www.lubbockonline.com/news/120696/inrussia.htm.

PricewaterhouseCoopers. n.d. *Doing Business in the Russian Federation.*

Rabushka, Alvin. 2002a. Tax Reform Remains High on Russia's Policy Agenda. Hoover Institution Public Policy Inquiry. May 22.
www.russianeconomy.org/comments/052202.html.

Rabushka, Alvin. 2002b. Improving Russia's 13% Flat Tax. Hoover Institution Public Policy Inquiry. March 11.
www.russianeconomy.org/comments/031102.html.

Rabushka, Alvin. 2002c. The Flat Tax at Work in Russia. Hoover Institution Public Policy Inquiry. February 21.
www.russianeconomy.org/comments/022102.html.

Rabushka, Alvin and Pauline Ryan. 1982. *The Tax Revolt.* Stanford: Hoover Institution Press.

Shleifer, Andrei and Daniel Treisman. 2000. *Without a Map: Political Tactics and Economic Reform in Russia.* Cambridge, MA and London: The MIT Press.

Tolkushkin, A.V. 2001. *Istoriia nalogov v Rossii* (Moscow: Iurist), p. 264.

Chapter 7

ACCOUNTING EDUCATION IN RUSSIA*

Abstract

Russia is in the process of converting its accounting system from the old Soviet model to one that resembles the systems found in developed market economies. The country is adopting international financial reporting standards but with a Russian flavor. To make the transition successful it is necessary to transform accounting education. Present practitioners must be educated in the new system and a new generation of accountants must learn the new system. This paper reviews the relevant accounting education literature and summarizes the results of interviews of accounting educators conducted in Russia during the summer of 2003.

INTRODUCTION

Accounting has been going through rapid changes in Russia ever since the Russian Finance Ministry decided to replace the country's centrally planned accounting system with a market based system in the early 1990s. A whole generation of accounting practitioners needed to change to a new system they knew nothing about – 1.5 million, according to one estimate (Smirnova et al. 1995). There were no textbooks or educational materials available in the Russian language. There were no teachers to teach the new system. Universities had to start teaching the new system to a new generation of students but their professors never studied the new system they were being asked to teach.

A decade has passed since the changes were initiated. There are now some accounting materials available in the Russian language that practitioners, students and professors can refer to but the quantity and quality of these publications leave something to be desired. Some accounting practitioners have learned the new rules while others have not. Some professors are now teaching International Financial Reporting Standards (IFRS) to their students while others continue to teach the old accounting system they learned decades ago as students. In short, the movement to reform accounting education is a

---

* An earlier version of this chapter was presented at the Academy of International Business – Southeast, Annual Conference, Clearwater, Florida, November 13-14, 2003.

mixed success. Although progress has been made in the last decade, much work remains to be done.

This chapter focuses on university accounting education in Russia. Other papers have taken a look at accounting education in the private sector and accounting certification (Preobragenskaya and McGee 2004a, b, c; McGee, Preobragenskaya and Tyler 2004a, b).

REVIEW OF THE LITERATURE

Much has been written about accounting reform in transition economies in general (Wallace 1993) and about Central and East European countries in particular (Richard 1998; Kemp & Alexander 1996; Garrod & McLeay 1996; Jermakowicz & Rinke 1996; Rolfe & Doupnik 1995). Some articles and book chapters have focused on accounting reform in particular East European countries and former Soviet republics, including Armenia (McGee 1999a, b), Belarus (Pankov 1998; Sucher & Kemp 1998), the Czech and Slovak Republics (Zelenka et al. 1996; Seal et al. 1995), Hungary (Borda & McLeay 1996; Boross et al. 1995), Lithuania (Mackevicius et al. 1996), Poland (Adams & McMillan 1997; Krzywda et al. 1996 & 1995), Romania (Roberts 2001; King et al 2001), Slovenia {Turk & Garrod 1996) and Uzbekistan (Crallan 1997).

Several studies have been made of accounting reform in Russia. Enthoven et al (1998) wrote a book covering accounting, auditing and taxation in Russia. Enthoven (1999; 1992) has also written about accounting reform in Russia in general. Shama and McMahan (1990) wrote about how perestroika was likely to change the nature of accounting in Eastern Europe and the former Soviet Union. Preobragenskaya and McGee (2003) discussed recent changes in auditing. Ramcharran (2000) wrote about the need for accounting harmonization regarding Russian banks. The International Center for Accounting Reform in Moscow has published a number of studies on accounting reform in Russia, including *Accounting Reform Recommendations* (2000) and also has a newsletter on the topic.

Most studies have discussed the transformation process in transition economies or the adoption and implementation of market based financial reporting rules. However, a few authors have written specifically about accounting education in transition economies. Lin and Deng (1992) reviewed the history and the then current situation of accounting education in China and made suggestions for the development and reform of Chinese accounting education. However, their study is more than ten years old and much has changed in Chinese accounting education since then. Chan and Rotenberg (1999) provide more recent information. However, their article is mostly concerned with other aspects of Chinese accounting and only touches on accounting education in China. The International Federation of Accountants published a Study Paper (IFAC 2000) on accounting education in developing countries and published guidelines for implementation of IFAC educational standards (2001). These IFAC publications have been used to provide guidance to educational leaders in several transition economies.

A few studies have addressed accounting education in Eastern Europe and the former Soviet republics. McGee did studies of accounting education reform in Armenia (2003a) and Bosnia and Herzegovina (2003b). Enthoven et al. (1998) devote a short chapter to accounting education in Russia in their book on accounting, auditing and taxation in Russia. However, their study is mostly an overview and was published in 1998. Much has changed since then.

Smirnova et al. (1995) published a more comprehensive study of Russian accounting education and provide a good summary of the state of accounting education shortly after the transition process began. Kobrak (1991) discussed the rapid increase in the demand for Western accounting textbooks after the Russian Ministry of Finance decided to adopt International Accounting Standards (IAS) in the early 1990s. Other articles discuss some of the weaknesses in Russian accounting education (Anon. 1994), the benefits to be gained by educational exchange programs (Coyle and Platonov 1998) and CIMA certification (Anon. 2001).

METHODOLOGY

After reviewing the literature on accounting reform in transition economies and accounting education in Eastern Europe and the former Soviet republics, the authors developed a tentative list of questions to ask Russian accounting educators. A sample of accounting educators representing state universities and the private sector was then selected and contacted. Interviews were scheduled and held during the summer and fall of 2003 in Moscow, St. Petersburg and elsewhere. Interviews were held at the following organizations:

Deloitte & Touche, Moscow office [www.deloitte.ru]
KPMG, Moscow office [www.kpmg.ru]
KPMG, St. Petersburg office [www.kpmg.ru]
PricewaterhouseCoopers, Moscow office [www.pwcglobal.com/ru]
Ajour, a Russian auditing and consulting firm, Moscow [www.ajour.ru]
PKF(MDK), a Russian audit and consulting firm, St. Petersburg office [www.mcd-pkf.com]
Independent Directors Association, Moscow [www.independentdirector.ru]
MDM Group, Moscow [www.mdmgroup.ru]
St. Petersburg State Polytechnic University [www.spbstu.ru]
St. Petersburg State Railway University (a.k.a. Petersburg State Transport University) [www.pgups.ru]
Timiryazev Agricultural Academy, Moscow [www.timacad.ru]

Hock Accountancy Training, Moscow office [www.hocktraining.com]
Omsk State University [www.omsu.omskreg.ru]
Kazan State Finance Economic Institute [www.kfei.kcn.ru]

Although many of the interviews were held in Russia's cultural capital (St. Petersburg) and political capital (Moscow), the authors did not want to limit the information gathering process to the two most economically advanced cities in Russia because doing so might result in a biased sample, so some interviews were conducted in more typical Russian cities (Omsk and Kazan) as well. This turned out to be a good decision, since accounting education, the level of accounting sophistication and the attitude toward the need for accounting proved to be different once one leaves Russia's two main cities.

ACCOUNTING AS A PROFESSION

The first commercial college was established in St. Petersburg in 1773. Between then and 1917, the number of commercial colleges offering accounting increased to 219. Moscow and Kiev also became centers for accounting education (Enthoven 1998).

The accounting system a country has is generally closely correlated to its culture and level of economic development. The accounting system a country has closely reflects the economic system a country has. The accounting system a developing economy has will be different and less sophisticated than the system a developed country has. A country with a centrally planned economy will require a different kind of accounting system than country that has a market economy (Choi et al. 2002).

The accounting system is generally not the driver of change. A flexible accounting system can adapt to changes taking place in the economy and society, but it is usually a follower, not a leader. Russia is not an exception. By 1917, Russia's accounting system was not much different from those of most Western countries (Enthoven et al. 1998: 1). After the communist revolution (1917), its accounting system adapted to meet the needs of a centrally planned economy. The system emphasized the collection of information for the government. Accounting was used as a tool for state control.

After perestroika and the opening up of the Russian economy and the adoption of market methods of resource allocation, Russia's accounting system had to change. And it did, but only grudgingly. The accounting system could no longer be just an instrument of state control. It also had to be a tool of business communication. The importance of financial information increased and the accountant's role changed in the new economic environment. Managers expect more from accountants now than before.

Accountants are expected not only to provide facts and details but also to make decisions that affect the company's business and even its survival.

As a consequence, the attitude toward the accounting profession has changed. A survey of secondary school graduates that was conducted before perestroika ranked accounting 91st out of 92 occupations (Enthoven et al. 1998: 199; Smirnova et al. 1995: 834). Accounting was a low paid and not well regarded occupation. People who worked in accounting were not even called accountants. They were called bookkeepers, which was a good description of what they actually did, since most of what they did would be called bookkeeping by Western standards. Although it was possible to study accounting in a university, many people who trained to become accountants received their training from vocational schools and received a diploma after two or three years (Smirnova et al. 1995).

All that changed after perestroika. A more recent survey (Anon. 2003) ranked accounting third among all professions. Although it is still possible to study accounting in a vocational school, an increasing number of universities are offering accounting courses and even accounting majors. Before perestroika, students who studied accounting in a university usually graduated with a degree in economics. There was no such thing as an accounting major at many universities, although there were some exceptions. Some universities still do not offer an accounting major, although the trend is to offer more accounting courses as well as four-year and five-year degrees in accounting.

UNIVERSITY EDUCATION

The number of Russian universities that teach accounting students has increased in the last ten years. Many universities that never before offered accounting courses are offering whole educational programs in accounting. From Table 1 it can be seen that 26.6% of the universities in Russia now teach accounting. This percentage may not seem very high by American standards since, in America, practically all universities offer accounting courses. But this percentage is much higher now in Russia than it was ten years ago, and it is likely to get even larger in the years to come.

Table 1 includes data from four Russian cities and Russia as a whole. Moscow and St. Petersburg are included because they are the two main cities in Russia. But they are not typical. That is why the authors decided to also include two more typical Russian cities – Omsk and Kazan – in the Table. Each of these typical Russian cities has more than a million population. In this paper they represent the rest of Russia. One reason Omsk was chosen is because it is the home city of one of the authors, which made it a convenient place to conduct interviews. Kazan was chosen because it is a typical Russian city and also because one of the authors had to be in Kazan on business anyway, which made it convenient to conduct interviews.

Table 1
Russian Universities Offering Accounting 2002

	Omsk	Kazan	St. Petersburg	Moscow	All Russia
1. Total number of universities	28	27	108	243	1898
2. Universities offering accounting courses	6	6	25	53	506
3. Percentage of universities offering accounting courses (Row2/Row1)	21.4%	22.2%	23.1%	21.8%	26.6%
4. Universities offering accounting courses that have state accreditation	2	5	10	30	239
5. Percentage of universities offering accounting that are accredited (Row4/Row2)	33.3%	83.3%	40%	56.6%	47.2%

Source: www.edu.ru

According to the law On Education, only those universities that receive state accreditation for certain educational programs (accredited programs) have a right to issue State Diplomas (certificates of degree). As can be seen from Table 1, only 26.6% of all Russian universities offer accounting courses, and only 47.2% of the Russian universities that offer accounting courses have this accreditation.

This percentage may seem low to American and Western European readers since, in American and Western European universities, practically every university offers accounting courses. But such is not the case in Russia. Part of the difference is accounted for by the fact that, traditionally, Russia had many institutes that were devoted to just a few subjects in some specialty area. Usually, the area of specialty did not include accounting. As these institutes began to adopt the name "university" for prestige reasons, they more or less maintained their prior curriculum. If they did not offer accounting courses before the name change, they did not offer accounting courses after the name change either. Also, as was previously mentioned, accounting was not a prestigious or popular major under the Soviet regime. It was only after perestroika and the opening up of the Russian economy to the market system that accounting became popular as well as increasingly important.

Of the 506 universities that offer accounting courses, 174 (34.5%) are private. The rest are state universities. Most of the 174 private universities were founded within the last 15 years or so, after perestroika started.

University education in Russia is much different than university education in the United States. Whereas in the USA, students have a large selection of electives to choose from, Russian accounting students have practically no choice in the courses they take. Once they choose to enroll in the accounting program, almost all courses are mandatory. They have few elective options.

The law On High and Post-university Education establishes the rules for the following higher education programs: Bachelor Degree (4 years), Specialist (5 years) and Masters Degree. At present, less than 10 percent of all Russian universities offer bachelor's and master's degree programs in accounting. The majority of universities offer the five-year specialist program. There are several reasons. For one, the five-year apprenticeship has been widely used in Russia for several decades and it is the program that Russian employers are most familiar with. Also, a student with only a bachelor's degree will not be as marketable as someone who completes a five-year program.

The six-year apprenticeship with the master's degree is not advantageous for universities because university budgets only provide for the five-year program. In most cases the State will not provide funding for the sixth year, so universities have little economic incentive to offer six-year master's programs. Also, employers do not place much extra value on the master's degree, so students have little incentive to study for an additional year.

During the course of the interviews it was discovered that the main reasons why students decide to continue their education for the sixth year are because:

- In the case of getting a post-graduate education, some courses taken as part of the master's program are counted as post-graduate hours;
- Students who plan to work abroad find that the master's degree makes them more marketable than having just the Specialist degree; and
- An extra year of study provides an additional delay from the Army.

Thus, at Saint Petersburg State Polytechnic University, for example, only 20 percent of their graduates continue studying for the sixth year.

In this paper we discuss students who major in accounting and who choose accounting as a profession. However, many universities that do not offer an accounting major offer accounting courses to managers, engineers and others and provide introductory accounting courses to their students. The number of students studying accounting has risen dramatically in recent years. The rate of increase for accounting students is greater than the rate of increase for total students studying in universities, which means that accounting students comprise a larger percentage of the total student population now than was the case a few years ago. Table 2 shows that the number of students studying accounting increased by 82.6% from 1998 to 2001, compared to an increase in the general student population of only 43.3%.

Table 2
**Growth in the Number of Students Studying Accounting
In Russian Universities 1998-2001**

	1998	1999	2000	2001
1. All students in all universities (thousands)	3347.2	3728.1	4270.1	4797.4
2. Increase compared to prior year /with 1998		11.4%	14.5%	12.3% /43.3%
3. Tuition paying students (thousands)	728.7	1021.3	1468.3	1954.6
4. Percentage of students who pay tuition (Row 3/Row 1)	21.8%	27.4%	34.4%	40.7%
5. Number of accounting students (thousands)	155.1	187.9	241.4	283.2
6. Increase compared to prior year /with 1998		21.1%	28.4%	17.3% /82.6%
7. Tuition paying accounting students (thousands)	69.9	98.8	148.8	187.2
8. Percentage of accounting students who pay tuition (Row 7/ Row 5)	45.1%	52.6%	61.6%	66.1%

Source: www.edu.ru

From Table 2 we can also see that the percentage of students paying for their education in Russia in 2001 was 40.7% and that the percentage of accounting students paying for their education in 2001 was 66.1%. It may seem strange that such statistics are even compiled since, in American universities, practically all students pay at least some tuition. But on the other hand, in some Western European countries university education is free. In some countries, the government even gives students a stipend for living expenses. That is one reason why students in some Western European countries take so long to graduate.

The situation in Russia is changing. Whereas university education used to be free or almost free, there is now a trend to charge tuition at least to some students. Tuition is especially important for the many private universities that are popping up all over Russia but it is also important for State universities, since the government cannot provide all the funding that universities need to continue operating.

One reason for the increase in the number of students studying accounting is because they are willing and able to pay tuition. That has enabled Russian universities to expand their accounting curriculum and it is one reason why some universities that formerly did not offer accounting courses are now offering them. One explanation for why the percentage of accounting students paying tuition is higher than the percentage of students in general who pay tuition is because accounting has become a more prestigious profession. Students are more willing to pay for such an education.

An accounting education is also one of the most expensive in Russia. On average it's about US$1000-1200 per year, which may seem low by American standards, but for Russia it is a tidy sum. In Omsk, only courses in international business and law are more expensive. Such a segmented tuition policy may seem strange to American educators, since American universities charge the same amount per credit hour regardless of which major a student chooses, but in Russia market forces have more influence on the level of tuition charged.

It must also be mentioned that another reason for the increase in the number of accounting students in Russia is part-time and distance education. Table 3 shows the percentage of full-time day students as a percentage of total students, both for all majors and for accounting majors.

Table 3
Full-time Day Students as a Percentage of Total Students
1998-2001

	1998	1999	2000	2001
1. Percentage of full-time day students as a percentage of students in all categories (All students in all universities)	60.9%	59.4%	57.2%	55.4%
2. Percentage of full-time day students as a percentage of students in all categories (Accounting students)	33.7%	31.3%	28.4%	27.3%

Source: www.edu.ru

It is thought that university day programs provide a better quality education than part-time evening or distance education programs. This belief has some basis in fact. Potential employers mention in their job ads that they seek to hire specialists with diplomas from day programs. That being the case, one cannot say much positive about the statistics given in Table 3. Accounting students tend to be full-time day students less often than students from other disciplines. Only 27.3 percent of the accounting students who completed their accounting degree in 2001 were day students, compared to 55.4 percent for the general student population.

On the other hand, attending university part-time evenings or by distance is often the only way for some students to obtain a university diploma. Sometimes a university diploma is required to retain one's job. Some people are afraid of losing their present position if they do not pursue a diploma. This is especially true of government positions. Both the universities and their students realize the fact that students are spending their time, money and effort not because they want to obtain knowledge (part-time and distance students are often more experienced and competent than their professors) but because they need a diploma. This understanding adversely affects the quality of distance education.

One factor that affects the quality of education is the quality of the professors who are teaching the students. The professors' qualifications, how well they are able to convey knowledge, how up to date they are with recent developments in their field, how high their teaching loads are, etc., all have an effect on the quality of the education students receive. According to the statistical data on the educational site www.edu.ru, the number of teaching staff in Russian universities in 2001 totaled 252.6 thousand, of which 44 percent had the title of professor or assistant professor. In addition, there were 50.4 thousand external moonlighters. The age distribution of the teaching staff in 2001 was distributed as follows: 31.4% under age 40, 47.1% between 40-59 and 21.5% over 59.

At present, the salary of professors is lower than the salaries of most other professions. The average university teacher's salary is 2500-5000 rubles per month, or about $83-$167, or $7 per hour of lecture. It must also be mentioned that the hourly rate of the economics department's professors (that is the department where accounting professors teach) is about twice as high as that of professors in other departments. Part of this differential is because of the laws of supply and demand and part is because accounting students pay a fee for this education, which provides the fund needed to pay this additional cost. In many universities the funds received from teaching economics (including accounting) are redistributed to other departments to support programs that do not generate as much money as the economics department.

The wages paid in universities cannot be compared to the wages paid in business. As a result, most of the professors who can market themselves as financial specialists have left the universities for the private sector. Those who remain in the universities obtain most of their income from outside sources rather than teaching. The majority work in consulting. Many have their own companies.

Why does anyone continue to teach accounting when practically any other field of endeavor pays more money? The prestige of being a university professor is one reason. Sometimes this prestige can be turned into cash in the private sector. There is a certain aura of credibility associated with being a university professor. Also, being at a university can be a source of clients, since some businesses apply directly to universities for help. Traditionally, universities have accumulated the best professionals in the field, so businesses tend to gravitate to the universities when they need assistance. Then there is the intangible aspect of the job, the fun and pleasure that are derived from giving lectures that has no substitute in the marketplace.

Universities welcome a teacher who is also a practitioner. It is believed, and rightly so in many cases, that someone who has current knowledge in the field is able to provide better, more practical and valuable lectures than someone who is a book-scientist. The downside of hiring practitioners is that they may not have much energy left to teach after they have spent all their time and energy during the day engaging in business activities. Also, as practitioners, they may not spend a sufficient amount of time in study, which is necessary to keep current in the field.

The huge increase in the demand for accounting education has led to an equal increase in the demand for people who can teach accounting. Meanwhile, professors have been leaving the university to go to the private, profit making sector, which has intensified the need for professors. Universities that formerly did not offer accounting courses have an especially difficult time trying to find people to teach the courses they recently started offering. These factors all have an effect on the quality of the education that accounting students receive.

THE SYLLABUS

In order to discuss the accounting education that Russian students receive it is necessary to look at the syllabus. In 2000 the Higher Education Ministry approved The State Educational Standard for the specialty "Accounting, Analysis and Audit," which provides guidelines on preparing specialists for the qualification of "economist." The main provisions of that Standard are outlined below. According to the Standard, the primary categories of a graduate's professional activities include the following: transaction accounting and analysis; revision; auditing; consulting; controlling; and methodical work. Applicants for entrance to the university need a secondary education or secondary professional education. The Fundamental Educational Program (FEP) includes curriculum, programs of the discipline and programs for educational and practical training. The program consists of a federal discipline component, a regional (university) component, some disciplines of the students' choice (elective courses) and some additional courses. The course is divided into the following categories:

General Humanities and Social Economics Disciplines (GH&SED)
General Mathematics and Natural Science Disciplines (GM&NSD)
General Professional Disciplines (GPD)
Special Disciplines (SD)
Additional Courses (AC)

Table 4 is an extract from Curriculum and shows the allocation of hours among the various categories.

Table 4
Allocation of Hours among Subject Categories

	Disciplines (including practice)	Total Hours	Percentage of Total
GH&SED	General Humanities and Social Economics Disciplines	1800	19.4%
GM&NSD	General Mathematics and Natural Science Disciplines	1400	15.1%
GPD	General Professional Disciplines	2200	23.7%
SD	Special Disciplines	2790	30.1%
AC	Additional Courses	1090	11.7%
	Totals	9280	100%

The period of study for the Fundamental Educational Program (FEP) for the day program is 260 weeks and consists of:

- Theoretical study (including scientific research, practical class training and exams) 186 weeks
- Practical training (in real companies) 16 weeks
- The final state exam, including work on a diploma project, not less than 11 weeks
- Vacations (including 8 weeks after-diploma vacation), not less than 47 weeks

The maximum load for a student cannot exceed 54 hours per week, including auditorium work time that should not be more than 27 hours per week. Universities are supposed to develop a FEP, using the Standard as the base. Specialization subjects are supposed to provide deep knowledge of certain kinds of businesses like bank accounting, accounting for nonprofit organizations, accounting for state organization, etc. Actual control and policies are established by the universities. The weight of grades given for interim results should not be less than 40 percent of the total grade. The remaining 60 percent is for the final examination. The main form of exam is a written test (not less than 70-75% of total tests). The grading scale is set by the university but for the final grade, scores must be converted into "excellent," "good," "satisfactory," and "unsatisfactory."

Universities have the flexibility to change the weighting of hours among the various categories by 5 percent. The contents of the General Humanities & Social Economics Disciplines category is set by each university but must include the following:

- Foreign languages – not less than 340 hours
- Physical training – not less than 408 hours
- Russian history and philosophy

At least 50 percent of the full-time professors must have the PhD. The final attestation includes the Diploma Project and the State Exam. Topics of Diplomas are determined by university departments. The State Exam includes questions about accounting, auditing and analysis. The State Exam is given by an examining board, which includes university representatives, professors from other universities and local authorities. The head of the board is usually from another university or a business professional.

Table 5 shows the ten subjects that accounting majors devote the most time to at St. Petersburg State Polytechnic University.

Table 5
Hours Devoted to the Top Ten Subjects

Rank	Discipline	Hours	%age
1	Foreign Languages	510	6.2%
2	Information Science	459	5.6%
3	Physical Training	408	5.0%
4	Mathematics	391	4.8%
5	Theory of Economics	357	4.3%
6	Financial Accounting	306	3.7%
7	Logistics	306	3.7%
8	Cost Accounting, budgeting for different industries	297	3.6%
9	Class Training (A case study of accounting of an enterprise activity)	264	3.2%
10	Concepts of Modern Natural Science	255	3.1%

Table 6 shows the ten subjects that accounting majors devote the least amount of time to.

Table 6
Hours Devoted to Lowest Ten Subjects

Rank	Discipline	Hours	%age
1	International Standards of Audit	48	0.6%
2	Vital Function Safety & Protection of Labor	68	0.8%
3	International Accounting Standards	85	1%
4	Russian History	85	1%
5	Finance	102	1.2%
6	Financial Statements and Analysis	102	1.2%
7	Pricing	102	1.2%
8	Insurance	102	1.2%
9	The Theory of Accounting	102	1.2%
10	Marketing	102	1.2%

From Table 6 it can be seen that several of the subjects having the least amount of time devoted to them are accounting. International Standards of Audit (ISA) has a mere 48 hours devoted to it. International Accounting

Standards is studied only 85 hours, although the Russian Finance Ministry has declared that Russian enterprises must follow IAS as of January 1, 2004, a full year before EU countries are required to adopt IAS. Finance, Financial Statements and Analysis and The Theory of Accounting are each allocated a mere 102 hours, even though they are included in the major.

Why are so few hours devoted to these very important subjects? The interviews conducted as part of this research uncovered several explanations. One reason mentioned before is the lack of teaching staff. It is difficult to find people who are qualified to give lectures in these subjects, especially outside of Russia's two main cities. Most potential accounting professors are in Moscow and St. Petersburg because that is where most of the sophisticated accounting is done. There is less demand for expertise on IAS and ISA outside of these two cities. There is grass roots demand for IAS and ISA expertise only among the large Russian enterprises that want to attract foreign capital, and those firms are located mostly in Moscow and St. Petersburg.

Another reason also has to do with economics. It was learned during the course of the interviews that accounting professors are twice as expensive as professors in other disciplines. Increasing the number of hours devoted to accounting subjects increases the university's costs, and there is pressure to keep costs down.

Another reason is the transformation in the structure of Russian universities. In Soviet times, most institutions of higher education were called institutes rather than universities. These institutes specialized in teaching just a few subjects. There is now a tendency to change the name from institute to university for reasons of prestige. With the name change comes a change in emphasis in the curriculum. These former institutes that are now universities have to teach more subjects but in less depth. There is now more emphasis on general subjects and less emphasis on whatever major subject the student chooses for a major.

Table 7 shows the breakdown of the five-year economist degree at St. Petersburg State Polytechnic University. The total program is subdivided into lectures, class study, laboratory study and self-study.

Table 7
Curriculum for Specialty "Accounting, Analysis and Audit"
St. Petersburg State Polytechnic University

Subjects	Number of Hours					Total	
	Lectures	Class Study	Lab. Study	Total Class Hours	Self Study	Hours	% of Total (8208 = 100%)
General Humanities and Social Economic Disciplines	**272**	**969**		**1241**	**561**	**1802**	**22.0%**

Federal Component	*170*	*901*		*1071*	*391*	*1462*	
Foreign Languages		340		340	170	510	6.2%
Physical Training		408		408		408	5.0%
Russian History	34	17		51	34	85	1.0%
Philosophy	34	34		68	34	102	1.3%
Economic Theory	102	102		204	153	357	4.3%
Regional (university) component	*102*	*34*		*136*	*102*	*238*	
Social Science	34			34	34	68	2.4%
Jurisprudence	68	34		102	68	170	2.1%
Electives		*34*		*34*	*68*	*102*	
Culture Science		34		34	68	102	1.3%
General Mathematics and Natural Sciences	**440**	**187**	**355**	**982**	**560**	**1542**	**18.8%**
Federal Component	*338*	*119*	*321*	*778*	*492*	*1270*	
Mathematics	119	119		238	153	391	4.8%
Information Science	85		204	289	170	459	5.6%
Information Systems in Economics	66		66	132	33	165	2.0%
Concepts of Modern Natural Science (Ecology)	68		51	119	136	255	3.1%
Regional (University) Component	*68*	*34*	*34*	*136*	*34*	*170*	
Econometrics	68	34	34	136	34	170	2.1%
Electives	*34*	*34*		*68*	*34*	*102*	
Probability Theory	34	34		68	34	102	1.2%
General Professional Disciplines	**758**	**369**	**153**	**1280**	**942**	**2222**	**27.1%**
Federal Component	*656*	*301*	*153*	*1110*	*721*	*1831*	
Economics of Enterprises	85		68	153	51	204	2.5%
Management	51	34		85	136	221	2.7%

Marketing	34	34		68	34	102	1.2%
Statistics	68		68	136	34	170	2.1%
World Economics	34	34		68	51	119	1.4%
Financial Management	68	17	17	102	34	136	1.8%
Finance	34	17		51	51	102	1.2%
Insurance	51	17		68	34	102	1.2%
Cash, Loan, Banks	48	32		80	48	128	1.6%
Stock Exchange Market	48	32		80	96	176	2.1%
Taxes	51	34		85	51	136	1.8%
The Theory of Accounting	34	17		51	51	102	1.2%
International Accounting Standards	34	17		51	34	85	1.0%
International Standards of Audit	16	16		32	16	48	0.6%
Regional (University) Component	*34*	*34*		*68*	*153*	*221*	
Business Communications (Contracts)	34	34		68	153	221	2.7%
Electives	*68*	*34*		*102*	*68*	*170*	
Pricing	34	17		51	51	102	1.2%
Vital Functions Safety & Protection of Labor	34	17		51	17	68	0.8%
Special Disciplines	**539**	**269**	**201**	**1009**	**1157**	**2166**	**26.4%**
Financial Accounting	85	34	34	153	153	306	3.7%
Management Accounting	51	34		85	51	136	1.7%
Financial Statement Analysis	34	17		51	51	102	1.3%
Complex Economic Analysis of enterprise Activity	68	34	34	136	102	238	2.9%
Audit	68	51		119	119	238	2.9%

Class Training (A case study of accounting of an enterprise activity)			82	82	182	264	3.2%
Electives	*48*	*16*		*64*	*96*	*160*	
Investment Analysis/Real Estate Economics	48	16		64	96	160	1.9%
Specialization Discipline	*185*	*83*	*51*	*319*	*403*	*722*	
Cost Accounting, Budgeting for Different Industries	66	66		132	165	297	3.6%
Accounting, Analysis and Audit of Foreign Economic Activity	34	17		51	68	119	1.5%
Logistics	85		51	136	170	306	3.7%
Practical Training							
Additional Courses		**476**		**476**		**476**	**5.7%**
TOTAL (hours)	2009	2270	709	4988	3220	8208	100%
Army Course		476		476		476	
TOTAL	**2009**	**2746**	**709**	**5464**	**3220**	**8684**	

OTHER ASPECTS OF ACCOUNTING EDUCATION

In the above example, 60.8% of all hours is devoted to class lessons. This percentage may be broken down into lectures (24.5%), auditorium lessons (27.7%) and laboratory practice (8.6%). The remaining 39.2% is devoted to self-study.

Practical training in companies is a component of the study process. Students are supposed to gain practical working knowledge by communicating with real business people. They learn how to work with accounting and business documents. They become acquainted with the accounting culture and environment. Traditionally, companies accepted students for a period of a few weeks to a few months and helped students achieve the required knowledge without compensation.

With the switch to a market economy companies' attitudes have changed. They now rarely agree to spend their employees' time helping students without being compensated for it. Also, allowing access by outsiders to company records is not in accord with the company's information security policy. Thus, obtaining practical knowledge has become a real problem for students as well as for universities.

One solution is a training "accounting class," which has been developed by the accounting department of Ural State Economic University. There are a few learning-work places and students can engage in accounting practice like real professionals.

Another important aspect of a university accounting education is textbooks. Over the last 15 years the content of accounting textbooks has changed dramatically. Accounting approaches have also gone through a transformation. It used to be that accounting textbook authors, along with providing knowledge of definitions, techniques and organizational matters paid a lot of attention to management accounting issues, although that term was not used. It was referred to as "calculation of the cost of production."

In the modern textbooks that are most widely used by accounting students, the main stress is now made on normative documents (legislation). This is not to say that all Russian accounting books place this emphasis but only those texts most likely to be found in university libraries. Much attention is focused on accounting documents, including how to fill them out and how to produce them. The textbooks often make it appear that the form and content of the documents is more important than the transactions themselves. As a consequence, most Russian accounting textbooks are more like collections of instructions and provisions that are current as of the date of publication. However, accounting textbooks sometimes get out of date quickly, and some of them are already out of date by the time they are published.

Society's (and clients') assessment of an accountant's professionalism is based on his or her knowledge of the laws, instructions and provisions they learned using those textbooks, as well as what they learned from their other university classes. Likewise, the universities attempt to meet market demand by producing graduates who have these characteristics and knowledge bases.

In general, it's great if an accountant (or even a student) can remember all the laws and is able to refer to a certain paragraph of instructions while analyzing a transaction. But there are major problems with this approach because Russian laws and instructions change so rapidly that much of what a student learns is outdated by the time they graduate and a high percentage of the normative documents that students have learned to use have become outdated.

Again, it should be emphasized that not *all* Russian textbooks fit this description; it is only the most widely used textbooks and the ones most likely to be found in university libraries that fit this description. As a consequence of this situation, many Russian professors develop their own textbooks and manuals and use them as the basis for teaching their students. Thus, like in many universities, Kazan State Finance Economy Institute, one of the most prestigious economic universities in Kazan, gives students the opportunity to study accounting using their professor's textbook (Kulikova 1999).

Russian accounting students generally do not buy new textbooks like is so often done in the USA and Western Europe. The reason is because textbooks are expensive and students cannot afford them. Instead, they go to the library and use whatever textbooks they can find. In some cases, universities have ways to subsidize the cost of student texts. That is the case for the Timiryazev Agricultural Academy in Moscow, for example. The Agricultural Ministry provides funds to subsidize the cost of textbooks so that a text might cost students just 60 rubles ($2).

CONCLUDING COMMENTS

It will take time for market economy logic to gain the upper hand over the still prevalent top-down system Russia has had for several generations. Instead of using accounting as a means of control for socialist property and as a tool for fulfilling a plan, users and providers of accounting information will have to see accounting as a tool for management decision making and control at the enterprise level. It will take time for accounting textbooks to reflect this new reality as well. Although several Western accounting textbooks have been translated into Russian, these books are generally unobtainable outside of Russia's two major cities. Also, the American examples in those texts to not always closely correspond to the Russian situation.

Sadly, the quality of Russian textbooks has declined during the last three generations. After the communist revolution, accounting texts began with V. Lenin quotations and contained inserts from the last Communist Party Congress Decree, but did not include definitions of capital, profit and the main accounting equation. It is a sad state of affairs, considering that pre-revolutionary accounting texts were at the level of those in Western market economies. They included not just theoretical chapters but also exercises and cases and intended to make students think, analyze and make decisions. They led students from the start of a transaction to the financial statements, taking into account who is the main user of accounting information and the purpose of accounting (Lihachev 1918).

There is a cultural dimension in Russian accounting that cannot easily be changed merely by issuing decrees or passing laws. Russian accounting is not based on concepts or principles. It is based on rules. The Russian mentality after generations of communist central planning is focused on instructions and rules, not principles. When Russian accountants encounter a problem, they do not think of how accounting principles can be used to arrive at a solution. They look for some written rule, instruction or law that addresses the issue. It is difficult to change this legalistic and formalistic approach to accounting.

There is still the widespread perception that accounting information is used primarily by tax officials and that it has little use for enterprise managers or potential investors. This attitude is also the result of the prior system and will change only slowly, with the passage of time. The new generation of accountants must learn how to make decisions based on accounting principles and professional judgment and must focus more on what is important to external users. The mentality of both students and professors must change in this regard before accounting education can achieve results approximating those of the more developed Western countries.

We have attempted to cover all the major factors that affect accounting students and graduates as they prepare to be professional accountants. What can be said to summarize the research and interviews? One interesting point that can be made is that those who were interviewed were in wide disagreement regarding the state of Russian accounting education. Some were quite optimistic and thought Russian accounting education was quite good and was improving rapidly. Others were pessimistic and thought that Russian accounting education was at a very low level. Some of those interviewed thought that graduates had a good knowledge of accounting while others thought the level of their knowledge left much to be desired.

Both of these views have some merit. Much depends on where the student studies and who the student's professors are. Those who study accounting in Moscow or St. Petersburg have a higher probability of having professors who have actually read and used IFRS, since universities outside of these two cities take a different approach and have a different attitude about the need to teach IFRS. Professors from other Russian cities also are not as well prepared or knowledgeable and the level and quality of materials available to students is also not as good.

Generally, the interviewees who were knowledgeable about International Financial Reporting Standards (IFRS) were more negative about the current state of Russian accounting education than were those who had merely heard about IFRS but had never read them. It is reasonable to expect that the quality of accounting education will eventually improve in the regions outside of Moscow and St. Petersburg, but this improvement in the quality of accounting education will be a bottom-up, market driven phenomenon rather than top-down, decree driven. Accounting education in Russia will improve as more high quality materials become available and as more accounting graduates gain experience and return to the universities to share their experience with the younger generation.

REFERENCES

Adams, Carol A. and Katarzyna M. McMillan, 1997. Internationalizing Financial Reporting in a Newly Emerging Market Economy: The Polish Example, *Advances in International Accounting* 10: 139-164.

Anonymous, 2003. Teaching in Russia, #2 (February), www.ht/prof/rang/rang_prof.html.

Anonymous, 2001. Accountants in Russia Gain International Skills, *Financial Management* (London) (April) 44.

Anonymous, 1994. Tanya Bondarenko Seeks American Education, *Baylor Business Review* 12(1): 12-14.

Borda, Maria and Stuart McLeay, 1996. Accounting and Economic Transformation in Hungary, in Neil Garrod and Stuart McLeay, editors, *Accounting in Transition: The Implications of Political and Economic Reform in Central Europe*, London and New York: Routledge 116-140.

Boross, Z., A.H. Clarkson, M. Fraser and P. Weetman, 1995. Pressures and Conflicts in Moving towards Harmonization of Accounting Practice: the Hungarian Experience, *The European Accounting Review* 4(4): 713-737.

Chan, M.W. Luke and Wendy Rotenberg, 1999. Accounting, Accounting Education, and Economic Reform in the People's Republic of China, *International Studies of Management & Organization* 29(3): 37-53.

Choi, Frederick D.S., Carol Ann Frost and Gary K. Meek, 2002. *International Accounting*, fourth edition, Upper Saddle River, NJ: Prentice Hall.

Coyle, William H. and Vladimir V. Platonov, 1998. Insights Gained from International Exchange and Educational Initiatives between Universities: The Challenges of Analyzing Russian Financial Statements, *Issues in Accounting Education* (February) 13(1): 223-233.

Crallan, Jocelyne, 1997. Accounting Reform in the CIS, *Management Accounting* (January) 34.

Enthoven, Adolf J.H., 1999. Russia's Accounting Moves West, *Strategic Finance* 81(1): 32-37.

Enthoven, Adolf J.H., 1992. Accounting in Russia: From Perestroika to Profits, *Management Accounting* 74(4): 27-31.

Enthoven, Adolf J.H., Yaroslav V. Sokolov, Svetlana M. Bychkova, Valery V. Kovalev and Maria V. Semenova, 1998. *Accounting, Auditing and Taxation in the Russian Federation*, Montvale, NJ and Richardson, TX: Institute of Management Accountants and The Center for International Accounting Development, University of Texas at Dallas.

Garrod, Neil and Stuart McLeay, editors, 1996. *Accounting in Transition: The Implications of Political and Economic Reform in Central Europe*, London and New York: Routledge.

International Center for Accounting Reform, 2000. *Accounting Reform Recommendations*, Moscow: International Center for Accounting Reform [www.icar.ru].

International Federation of Accountants, 2001. Strategy for Implementation of IFAC International Education Guideline No. 9: "Prequalification Education, Tests of Professional Competence and Practical Experience of Professional Accountants:" A Task Force Report of The International Association for Accounting Education and Research (IAAER), (February), New York: International Federation of Accountants, available at www.ifac.org.

International Federation of Accountants, 2000. Assistance Projects in Accountancy Education and Development, A Study Based on the Experience of IFAC Member Bodies, Study Paper (February), New York: International Federation of Accountants, available at www.ifac.org.

Jermakowicz, Eva and Dolores F. Rinke, 1996. The New Accounting Standards in the Czech Republic, Hungary, and Poland vis-à-vis International Accounting Standards and European Union Directives, *Journal of International Accounting Auditing & Taxation* 5(1): 73-88.

Kemp, Peter and David Alexander, 1996. Accountancy and Financial Infrastructure in Central and Eastern European Countries, *European Business Journal* 8(4): 14-21.

King, N., A. Beattie and A.-M. Cristescu, 2001. Developing Accounting and Audit in a Transition Economy: The Romanian Experience, *The European Accounting Review* 10(1): 149-171.

Kobrak, Fred, 1991. Is There an Accounting Textbook Market in the New Soviet Union? *Publishers Weekly*, (September 29) 43-44.

Krzywda, Danuta, Derek Bailey and Marek Schroeder, 1996. The Impact of Accounting Regulation on Financial Reporting in Poland, in Neil Garrod and Stuart McLeay, editors, *Accounting in Transition: The Implications of Political and Economic Reform in Central Europe*, London and New York: Routledge 61-92.

Krzywda, Danuta, Derek Bailey and Marek Schroeder, 1995. A Theory of European Accounting Development Applied to Accounting Change in Contemporary Poland, *The European Accounting Review* 4(4): 625-657.

Kulikova, Lidia I. 1999. *Financial Accounting*, Kazan, Russia, second edition.

Law on Education, 10 July 1992, #3266-1.

Law on High and Post-university Education, 22 August 1996, #125 FZ.

Lihachev, V.N. 1918. *30 Lessons in Double Entry Bookkeeping*, Moscow: K.I. Tihimirov's Trade House, fourth edition.

Lin, Zhijun and Shengliang Deng, 1992. Educating Accountants in China: Current Experiences and Future Prospects, *International Journal of Accounting* 27(2): 164-77.

Mackevicius, Jonas, Juozas Aliukonis and Derek Bailey, 1996. The Reconstruction of National Accounting Rules in Lithuania, in Neil Garrod and Stuart McLeay, editors, *Accounting in Transition: The Implications of Political and Economic Reform in Central Europe*, London and New York: Routledge 43-60.

McGee, Robert W., 2003a. Reforming Accounting Education in a Transition Economy: A Case Study of Armenia, in Erdener Kaynak and Talha D. Harcar, editors, *Succeeding in a Turbulent Global Marketplace: Changes, Developments, Challenges and Creating Distinct Competencies*, Hummelstown, PA: International Management Development Association 139-146. Also available at WWW.SSRN.COM.

McGee, Robert W. 2003b. Educating Professors in a Transition Economy: A Case Study of Bosnia and Herzegovina, in Erdener Kaynak and Talha D. Harcar, editors, *Succeeding in a Turbulent Global Marketplace: Changes, Developments, Challenges and Creating Distinct Competencies*, Hummelstown, PA: International Management Development Association 155-162. Also available at WWW.SSRN.COM.

McGee, Robert W. 1999a.The Problem of Implementing International Accounting Standards: A Case Study of Armenia, *Journal of Accounting, Ethics & Public Policy* 2(1): 38-41. Also available at WWW.SSRN.COM.

McGee, Robert W. 1999b. Certification of Accountants and Auditors in the CIS: A Case Study of Armenia, *Journal of Accounting, Ethics & Public Policy* 2(2): 338-353. Also available at WWW.SSRN.COM.

McGee, Robert W., Galina G. Preobragenskaya and Michael Tyler. 2004a. International Accounting Certification in the Russian Language: A Case Study. Presented at the International Academy of Business and Public Administration Disciplines (IABPAD) Conference, Tunica, Mississippi, May 24-26. http://ssrn.com/abstract=538622.

McGee, Robert W., Galina G. Preobragenskaya and Michael Tyler. 2004b. English Language International Accounting Certification in the CIS, Eastern and Central Europe. Presented at the International Academy of Business and Public Administration Disciplines (IABPAD) Conference, Tunica, Mississippi, May 24-26. http://ssrn.com/abstract=538602.

Pankov, Dmitri, 1998. Accounting for Change in Belarus, *Management Accounting* (London) 76(10): 56-58.

Preobragenskaya, Galina G. and Robert W. McGee, 2003. The Current State of Auditing in Russia, in Jerry Biberman and Abbass F. Alkhafaji, editors, *Business Research Yearbook: Global Business Perspectives*, Vol. X, Saline, MI: McNaughton & Gunn, Inc. 499-503. Also available at WWW.SSRN.COM.

Preobragenskaya, Galina G. and Robert W. McGee. 2004a. Private Sector Accounting Education in Russia. Presented at the International Academy of Business and Public Administration Disciplines (IABPAD) Annual Conference, New Orleans, January 23-25. http://ssrn.com/abstract=480743

Preobragenskaya, Galina G. and Robert W. McGee. 2004b. International Accounting and Finance Certification in the Russian Federation. Presented at the 16th Annual Conference of the International Academy of Business Disciplines, San Antonio, Texas, March 25-28. http://ssrn.com/abstract=538722.

Preobragenskaya, Galina G. and Robert W. McGee. 2004c. Recent Developments in Private Sector Accounting Education in Russia. Presented at the 16th Annual Conference of the International Academy of Business Disciplines, San Antonio, Texas, March 25-28. http://ssrn.com/abstract=538642.

Ramcharran, Harri, 2000. The Need for International Accounting Harmonization: An Examination and Comparison of the Practices of Russian Banks, *American Business Review* 18(1): 1-8.

Richard, Jacques, 1998. Accounting in Eastern Europe: from communism to capitalism, in Peter Walton, Axel Haller and Bernard Raffournier, editors, *International Accounting*, London: International Thomson Business Press 295-323.

Roberts, Alan, 2001. The Recent Romanian Accounting Reforms: Another Case of Cultural Intrusion? in Yelena Kalyuzhnova and Michael Taylor, editors, *Transitional Economies: Banking, Finance, Institutions*, Basingstoke, UK and New York: Palgrave 146-166.

Rolfe, Robert J. and Timothy S. Doupnik, 1995. Accounting Revolution in East Central Europe, *Advances in International Accounting* 8: 223-246.

Seal, Willie, Pat Sucher and Ivan Zelenka, 1995. The Changing Organization of Czech Accounting, *The European Accounting Review* 4(4): 659-681.

Shama, Avraham and Christopher G. McMahan, 1990. Perestroika and Soviet Accounting: From a Planned to a Market Economy, *International Journal of Accounting* 25: 155-169.

Smirnova, Irina A., Jaroslav V. Sokolov and Clive R. Emmanuel, 1995. Accounting Education in Russia Today, *The European Accounting Review* 4(4): 833-846.

Sucher, Pat and Peter Kemp, 1998. Accounting and Auditing Reform in Belarus, *European Business Journal* 10(3): 141-147.

Turk, Ivan and Neil Garrod, 1996. The Adaptation of International Accounting Rules: Lessons from Slovenia, in Neil Garrod and Stuart McLeay, editors, *Accounting in Transition: The Implications of Political and Economic Reform in Central Europe*, London and New York: Routledge 141-162.

Wallace, R.S. Olusegun. 1993. Development of Accounting Standards for Developing and Newly Industrialized Countries, *Research in Third World Accounting* 2: 121-165.

Zelenka, Ivan, William Seal and Pat Sucher, 1996. The Emerging Institutional Framework of Accounting in the Czech and Slovak Republics, in Neil Garrod and Stuart McLeay, editors, *Accounting in Transition: The Implications of Political and Economic Reform in Central Europe*, London and New York: Routledge 93-115.

Chapter 8

ACCOUNTING AND FINANCE CERTIFICATION*

Abstract
The Russian Finance Ministry has announced that Russia will adopt International Financial Reporting Standards (IFRS) as of January 1, 2004, one full year ahead of the European Union. This move is intended to give Russian financial statements more credibility in international capital markets. The problem is that there are very few Russian accountants who possess a certification that is internationally recognized and respected, with the result that certified statements of Russian firms is close to meaningless. One exception is statements that are certified by one of the Big-Four international accounting firms, but those firms audit only a small subset of all Russian firms. It is possible to purchase an accounting certificate in Russia and there are several kinds of legitimate certificates in Russia that are relatively easy to obtain, in the sense that the rigor of the examination process is much less than that required to pass an international certification exam. The private sector is attempting to provide a solution to this lack of credibility by international certification. This paper reviews those efforts.

INTRODUCTION

The present paper evolved out of a larger research project that examined recent developments in accounting in the Russian Federation. During the summer of 2003 the authors interviewed representatives from the following organizations in Russia:

Deloitte & Touche, Moscow office [www.deloitte.ru]
KPMG, Moscow office [www.kpmg.ru]

---

* An earlier version of this chapter was presented at the 16th Annual Conference of the International Academy of Business Disciplines, San Antonio, March 25-28, 2004.

KPMG, St. Petersburg office [www.kpmg.ru]
PricewaterhouseCoopers, Moscow office [www.pwcglobal.com/ru]
Ajour, a Russian auditing and consulting firm, Moscow [www.ajour.ru]
PKF(MDK), a Russian audit and consulting firm, St. Petersburg office
    [www.mcd-pkf.com]
Independent Directors Association, Moscow [www.independentdirector.ru]
MDM Group, Moscow [www.mdmgroup.ru]
St. Petersburg State Polytechnic University [www.spbstu.ru]
St. Petersburg State Railway University (a.k.a. Petersburg State Transport
    University) [www.pgups.ru]
Timiryazev Agricultural Academy, Moscow [www.timacad.ru]
Hock Accountancy Training, Moscow office [www.hocktraining.com]
Omsk State University [www.omsu.omskreg.ru]
Kazan State Finance Economic Institute [www.kfei.kcn.ru]

During the course of the interviews a number of individuals commented on the lack of credibility of Russian financial statements and the low level of accounting certification in the Russian Federation. They also mentioned how the credibility problem is being dealt with. The credibility problem is compounded by the recent increase in demand for high quality accounting services.

The interviews confirmed what the literature said regarding the lack of credibility in Russian financial statements. A study by Rozhnova (2000) of 1,040 Russian accountants employed by business enterprises found several reasons why there is a lack of confidence in Russian financial statements. The main reasons were:

- Inappropriate regulatory (tax and legal) framework (88%)
- Frequent changes in laws and regulations (85%)
- Deliberate misrepresentation of accounting records (reluctance of enterprises to disclose public information) (51%)
- Inappropriate accounting laws and regulations (45%)

The Finance Ministry of the Russian Federation has announced that all Russian banks and many Russian corporations must start using International Financial Reporting Standards (IFRS) as of January 1, 2004, with a full transition to be completed by January 1, 2007 (Anon. 2003a, b). The problem with Russia's adoption of IFRS is that very few Russian accountants are sufficiently familiar with IFRS to be able to certify the statements of Russian enterprises (McGee and Preobragenskaya, 2004). This lack of local expertise is partially overcome by the Big-Four accounting firms, all of which have offices in Russia and all of which certify the financial statements of Russian firms. There are a few second-tier international accounting firms competing for the Russian market as well (Anon. 2003c).

The result of this lack of local expertise is a two-tier system. At the upper level, the Big-Four international accounting firms compete to win audit contracts of the twenty-five or fifty largest Russian corporations, since they are the enterprises that are most in need of attracting foreign direct investment (FDI). The local Russian accounting and audit firms have to be content with servicing the many smaller and medium size clients, which do not have the same need for FDI, and which, for the most part, issue financial statements based on Russian Accounting Standards (RAS). These local Russian firms employ accountants and auditors who possess Russian accounting and audit certificates.

There are several problems with Russian accounting and audit certification. One weakness is the fact that thee are several different kinds of certification, and potential foreign investors are not familiar with Russian certification, which causes them to place less confidence in financial statements that are certified by an accountant or auditor who possesses only a Russian certification. Another problem is that Russian certification is easier to obtain than several of the more highly recognized foreign certifications. Interviews conducted during the summer of 2003 in Russia revealed that Russian certification exams are perceived as being little more than university exams. They are perceived as being far less rigorous than those of several internationally recognized certifications.

Another problem with Russian certification that was revealed during the course of the interviews is that it is possible to buy some Russian certificates. Several groups that issue Russian certification travel around the country selling their certificates. A virtual plethora of certifications now exists in Russia, some valid and some not, and some requiring little more than payment. As a result, financial statements that are certified by Russian certified accountants lack credibility. This problem is compounded by the fact that the Russian government refuses to recognize or grant reciprocity to accountants who possess any of the various internationally recognized accounting certifications. The market is overcoming this problem. This paper discusses how this problem is being dealt with.

LITERATURE REVIEW

Not much has been written about accounting certification in transition or emerging economies in general or Russia in particular. McGee (1999a, b) has written about accounting certification in Armenia. The Armenian model transfers some of the responsibility for accounting certification from the finance ministry to the private sector. Armenia has adopted the ACCA syllabus for its certification model and grants reciprocity for individuals who pass the English language ACCA exams.

A very brief article mentions that some CIMA training is given in Russia but does not go into any detail (Anon. 2001). A USAID-funded project to establish regional accounting certification in five Central Asian republics and perhaps Ukraine and Moldova using a different model has been in existence for several years, but no scholarly articles have been published about the program. The authors learned of this program during the course of the interviews. The private firm that has the USAID contract (Pragma) was contacted but declined to provide any details about the program until after this paper was presented at a conference.

However, some information about this program is available on the internet. Enthoven (2003) mentions this program in a brief article. The United States Agency for International Development (USAID) website also provides some information about it. Some information provided by Pragma and USAID shortly before this book went to press has been published in conference proceedings (McGee, Preobragenskaya and Tyler 2004a, b). This program is discussed in more detail below.

The International Center for Accounting Reform (ICAR) Newsletter (1999) briefly mentions the need for an internationally recognized Russian accounting and auditing certification but does not go into any detail. ICAR also published a position paper on accounting reform that advocates International Accounting Standards (IAS) certification (2000) but only one sentence is devoted to the international certification issue. Burnham (2000) devotes one sentence to advocating an accounting certification program to be run by a private accounting association in Russia. Zhuravlev (2001) discusses the International Association of Bookkeepers (IAB) educational program in Russia.

THE AMERICAN CPA EXAM

The American Certified Public Accountant (CPA) designation is internationally recognized for quality and high standards. It is a rigorous exam with a low pass rate. Holders of the American CPA possess a high degree of credibility, since the certification cannot be bought but must be earned. Such a statement may seem obvious and hardly worthy of mention to readers from industrialized countries, but to Russians and residents of other East European and developing economies such an attribute is very important.

The American CPA certificate is perceived as being of higher quality than any certification recognized by the Russian government. Although the Russian government does not recognize the American CPA or any other foreign accounting certification, the market *does* recognize such certifications. Russians who are able to obtain the American CPA are able to get good jobs in the private sector. Thus, there is a demand for the American CPA in Russia. Private sector training organizations have popped up to provide training for Russian accountants who want to take the American CPA exam and Russians are signing up to take CPA exam preparation courses in several major Russian cities as well as cities in several former Soviet republics, including Ukraine and Kazakhstan.

Russians who want to take the American CPA exam face several obstacles, some of them major. For one, the CPA exam is given only in English, which precludes the majority of Russian accountants from considering this certification option. Another problem is that the American CPA exam is given only in the USA, which means that any Russian who wants to take the exam must fly to the USA and incur the cost of airfare, hotel and meals as well as pay the examination fees. These costs are quite high by Russian standards, yet many Russian accountants find ways to pay them anyway because of the perception that the American CPA is worth the investment. This problem will become worse as the CPA exam becomes available in computer format because it will be offered over several months rather than just two days. That means that Russian accountants who want to take the CPA exam may have to stay in the USA for more than a month to take all parts of the CPA exam, which will greatly increase their costs for meals and lodging.

Another problem with obtaining the American CPA is the fact that most states now require 150 semester hours of accounting education to sit for the exam. Many Russian accountants are graduates of four-year programs in Russian universities and thus do not have a sufficient number of courses. Also, many Russian universities do not offer the accounting courses needed to qualify for the American CPA exam, since many states require a higher number of accounting credits than Russian universities offer.

There are a few exceptions. For example, New Hampshire requires only 12 semester hours of accounting to sit for the CPA exam. Maine used to be another popular state for Russian accountants because it had a low entry barrier. But Maine recently raised its requirements to sit for the CPA exam, making it unavailable to many Russian accountants. The number of states that allow Russian accountants possessing the standard Russian accounting education to sit for the CPA exam is limited, thus decreasing the opportunity to avail oneself of this option.

THE CMA AND CFM EXAMS

Another option for Russian accountants who want to obtain a foreign accounting certification is the CMA and CFM. The Institute of Certified Management Accountants (ICMA) has been giving the Certified Management Accountant (CMA) exam since 1972 (IMA 2003). The first exams were given in the USA. The first international exam was given in the Netherlands in 1988 (ICMA 2003). The Certified in Financial Management (CFM) exam was added to the ICMA list of offerings in 1996, when the first CFM exams were offered both in the USA and abroad. The international program has expanded to the point where more than 38% of the candidates taking the CMA/CFM exams are outside of the United States.

The CMA and CFM exams can now theoretically be given wherever the Graduate Record Exam (GRE) and Test of English as a Foreign Language (TOEFL) exams are given, since the CMA and CFM exams are proctored by Prometric [www.prometric.com], the same organization that offers the GMAT and TOEFL in more than 60 countries. Here are some statistics furnished by the ICMA for the period March 10, 2002 to March 10, 2003.

Table 1 shows the number of registrations. Candidates in the United States account for the most registrations, 8,194 out of a total of 13,284 worldwide, or 61.7%. The United Arab Emirates is in second place with 621 registrations (4.7%). Russia Ranked #6 with 439 registrations and 3.3% of the total registrations.

Table 1
Registrations for the CMA/CFM Exams
March 10, 2002 to March 10, 2003

Rank	Country	Registrations	% of Total
1	United States	8,194	61.7%
2	United Arab Emirates	621	4.7
3	Saudi Arabia	510	3.8
4	Egypt	482	3.6
5	South Korea	459	3.5
6	Russia	439	3.3
7	Jordan	432	3.2
8	Netherlands	352	2.6
9	Canada	339	2.5
10	Japan	213	1.6
11	People's Republic of China	169	1.3
12	India	121	0.9
13	Hong Kong	117	0.9
14	Bahrain	83	0.6
15	Kuwait	80	0.6
16	Lebanon	75	0.6
17	Kazakhstan	36	0.3
18	Germany	22	0.2
	Other	540	4.1
	Total	13,284	100.0%

Source: ICMA

Table 2 summarizes the pass rates on the CMA/CFM exams by country for the same period. Germany ranked #1 with a pass rate of 72%, followed by the People's Republic of China, with a 67% pass rate, which is surprising, since the exams are given in English. One would expect that the countries achieving the highest pass rates would be countries where English is the first language. One explanation for the high pass rates achieved by non-English speaking countries would be that only the top students took the exam. Another explanation would be that only very motivated students took the exam. The two explanations are not mutually exclusive. The USA ranked #6 with a pass rate of 58%. Russia ranked #7 with a pass rate of 48%, which was better than the average for non-US countries (43%).

Table 2
Pass Rates on CMA/CFM Exams
March 10, 2002-March 10, 2003

Rank	Country	Pass Rate %age	Exam Parts Passed
1	Germany	72	16
2	People's Republic of China	67	113
3	India	66	80
4	Netherlands	65	229
5	Canada	59	200
6	USA	58	4,727
7	Russia	48	211
8	Hong Kong	46	54
9	South Korea	45	207
10	Bahrain	42	35
11	Kazakhstan	42	15
12	Kuwait	40	32
13	United Arab Emirates	36	224
14	Japan	35	75
15	Egypt	32	154
16	Saudi Arabia	31	158
17	Jordan	30	130
18	Lebanon	25	19
	Other	42	229
	Total		6,906
	Total International	43%	

Source: ICMA

Table 3 ranks the number of new CMAs/CFMs during the period per million population of each country. The population statistics are estimates as of July 2003 and were taken from the CIA World Facts internet site. The CIA site did not list Hong Kong, so the population for Hong Kong (2002) was taken from the Hong Kong Census and Statistics Department website. The results clearly show that none of the countries will soon be overrun with CMA or CFMs. However, there were some surprises. The United Arab Emirates was the clear winner with 10.8 new CMAs/CFMs per million population, followed by Bahrain with 7.1. Jordan was slightly ahead of the USA with 3.8. Russia was far down the list, in 15th place. However, 15th place is not so bad, considering there are about 200 countries in the world.

Table 3
New CMAs/CFMs
March 10, 2002-March 10, 2003

Rank	Country	New CMAs/CFMs	Total Population (millions)	New CMAs/CFMs per Million Population
1	United Arab Emirates	27	2.5	10.8000
2	Bahrain	5	0.7	7.1429
3	Jordan	21	5.5	3.8182
4	USA	1008	290.3	3.4723
5	Kuwait	5	2.2	2.2727
6	Netherlands	36	16.2	2.2222
7	Hong Kong	7	6.8	1.0294
8	Saudi Arabia	25	24.3	1.0288
9	Lebanon	3	3.7	0.8108
10	South Korea	26	48.3	0.5383
11	Canada	15	32.2	0.4658
12	Egypt	14	74.7	0.1874
13	Kazakhstan	2	16.8	0.1190
14	Japan	15	127.2	0.1179
15	Russia	15	144.5	0.1038
16	India	9	1049.7	0.0086
17	People's Republic of China	7	1287.0	0.0054
18	Germany	0	82.4	0.0000

Source: ICMA

Table 4 shows the exam locations in Russia and the other former Soviet republics. As of November 2003, seven of the 15 former Soviet republics had exam locations for the CMA/CFM exams. Russia was the only former Soviet republic that had more than one exam location.

Table 4
CMA/CFM Exam Locations
Russia and Other Former Soviet Republics
As of November 2003

Country	Cities
Armenia	Yerevan
Azerbaijan	None
Belarus	None
Estonia	None
Georgia	Tbilisi
Kazakhstan	Almaty
Kyrgyzstan	None
Latvia	None
Lithuania	Vilnius
Moldova	None
Russia	Moscow Novosibirsk St. Petersburg
Tajikistan	None
Turkmenistan	None
Ukraine	Kiev
Uzbekistan	Tashkent

Source: www.prometric.com

As of November, 2003 there were 21 CMAs and 11 CFMs in Russia (ICMA 2003).

ACCA EXAMS

The Association of Chartered Certified Accountants (ACCA) has been offering certification exams for more than 100 years. Originating in the UK, the ACCA now gives certification exams in more than 140 countries, making it the premier international accounting certification issuing body in the world. As of November 2003 the ACCA had well over 1,000 students registered for its exams in Russia and over 7,000 students registered in the whole of Central and Eastern Europe (ACCA 2003). Table 5 shows the ACCA exam locations in Russia and the other former Soviet republics as of November 2003. Exams are given in eight of the 15 former Soviet republics, but the exam centers and countries are not identical to those for the CMA/CFM exams.

Table 5
ACCA Exam Locations
Russia and Other Former Soviet Republics
As of November 2003

Country	Cities
Armenia	Yerevan
Azerbaijan	None
Belarus	None
Estonia	Tallinn
Georgia	None
Kazakhstan	Almaty
Kyrgyzstan	None
Latvia	Riga
Lithuania	Vilnius
Moldova	None
Russia	Moscow St. Petersburg Vladivostok
Tajikistan	None
Turkmenistan	None
Ukraine	Kiev
Uzbekistan	Tashkent

Source: www.accaglobal.com

ACCA exams are given at three levels. More than a dozen exams are given in all. Exams are given twice a year. There is also an experience requirement. It often takes three years or more to pass all of the exams.

There is an interesting story behind the reason why the ACCA exams are so popular in Russia. In 1997 Price Waterhouse was debating which international certification exam they would encourage their employees to take. The rival candidates were the American CPA exam and the British ACCA. The American Institute of Certified Public Accountants (AICPA) and their state counterparts were pushing to require 150 semester hours of university education (five years) to be eligible to take the CPA exam. The ACCA, on the other hand, only requires a university degree. The ACCA does not specify how long the degree program should take. In fact, many British universities offer a three-year bachelor's degree.

Most Russian certification candidates were not able to meet the new five-year rule for the CPA exam but were able to meet the less stringent ACCA degree requirement because many Russian university programs were less than five years in duration. Thus, Price Waterhouse chose to support the ACCA certification program.

THE CIPA EXAMS

This program is offered by the International Council of Certified Accountants and Auditors, a group that was founded in 2002 by twelve accounting organizations in Russia, Ukraine, Kazakhstan, the Kyrgyz Republic, Tajikistan, and Uzbekistan (Anon., 2003d). Their program tests on international accounting and auditing standards as well as other accounting subjects and is mutually recognized within the six named countries, thus making it a regional accounting certification. The title of the designation is Certified International Professional Accountant (CIPA). One attractive feature of this designation is that the exams are in the Russian language, which makes it available to many more accountants than the CPA, CMA, CFM and ACCA exams, which are available only in English.

The exams are given in two levels. Those who pass the level one exams will be called certified accounting practitioners (CAP). Those who pass level two will earn the CIPA designation. Enthoven (2003) reports that the pass rate on the first level one exams was more than 50 percent and that the first level two exams were to be given later in 2003, after the Enthoven article was published. The USAID website for the Central Asia project (USAID-Pragma) also has some information on this series of exams.

The first CAP exams were given in May 2002. The first CIPA exams were given in November 2002. About 10,000 individuals took part in the first two exams. More than 3,600 candidates from seven countries, including Russia took part in the first CIPA exams (Anon. 2003f). Table 6 shows the results of the November 2002 exams:

Table 6
CIPA Exam Results
November 2002

CAP Exams	Passes	Pass Rate
Financial Accounting 1	723	50%
Managerial Accounting 1	420	51%
Tax and Law	464	67%
CIPA Exams		
Audit	N/A	N/A
Financial Accounting 2	N/A	N/A

The first CAP certificates were awarded between January and March, 2003 to successful candidates in four Central Asian republics. Results for Russia and Ukraine were not reported (Anon., 2003e). Passing statistics were as follows:

Kyrgyzstan 108
Uzbekistan 40
Kazakhstan 156
Tajikistan 15

CIIA EXAM

The Association of Certified International Investment Analysts (ACIIA) [www.aciia.org] was founded in the UK in 2000 and is composed of independent federations and national societies in at least 22 countries. It offers the Certified International Investment Analyst (CIIA) exam in Russia and elsewhere. The exams may be taken in the Russian language as well as several other languages. Although not strictly an accounting certification, the exams test on several subjects that are related to accounting. The Common Knowledge exams are divided into two levels, the Foundation Level and the Final Level.

There are three exams at the Foundation Level, covering equity valuation and analysis, financial accounting and statement analysis, corporate finance, fixed income valuation and analysis, economics, derivative valuation and analysis, portfolio management. Foundation Level exams can be waived if candidates already have relevant qualifications.

The two Final Level exams test on corporate finance, economics, financial accounting and statement analysis, equity valuation and analysis, fixed income valuation and analysis, derivative valuation and analysis and portfolio management. There is also a three-hour national exam that varies depending on the country of the candidate. This exam tests on regulation, ethics, financial statement analysis and market structures and instruments.

CFA EXAM

The Association for Investment Management and Research [www.aimr.com] offers the Chartered Financial Analyst (CFA) exam in Moscow as well as Baku, Kiev, Riga, Vilnius and Almaty. The June 2002 exam was given to more than 101,000 people in more than 150 countries, making it a truly international exam. The exam was first given in 1963 in the United States and Canada. The exams are at three levels and test on the following subjects: ethical and professional standards, quantitative methods, economics, financial statement analysis, corporate finance, analysis of equity investments, analysis of fixed income investments, derivatives, alternative investments and portfolio management. The overall pass rate worldwide in 2002 was 47 percent (Johnson and Squires, 2003).

INTERNATIONAL ASSOCIATION OF BOOKKEEPERS EXAMS

The International Association of Bookkeepers [www.iab.org.uk] was formed in the UK in 1973 and provides certification exams in bookkeeping at several levels in more than 90 countries. The first exams were given in Russia in 1998. Exams are now given in Moscow, Saint Petersburg, Kazan, Yekaterinburg and Novosibirsk. Subjects covered include international accounting and management accounting in addition to bookkeeping. Exams are given in the Russian language (Zhuravlev 2001).

CONCLUDING COMMENTS

The lack of credible accounting certification in Russia is being dealt with by the market. Even though the Russian government refuses to recognize foreign accounting certifications, the marketplace *does* recognize quality foreign accounting certifications that have stood the test of time and that have established credibility in the international marketplace. The lack of official recognition by the Russian government is becoming increasingly irrelevant as more Russian accountants pass the various international certification exams.

The interviews found that practically all lower level and mid-level Russian accountants who work for one of the Big-Four accounting firms in Russia are either studying for one of the international certification exams or have already passed one or more international certification exams. The Big-Four accounting firms require it as a condition of long-term employment. Russian accountants who want to be promoted or retained by one of these large firms feel compelled to obtain an international certification. Most of them also have a Russian certification.

Russian enterprises that want to attract foreign direct investment gravitate to Russian enterprises that have their financial statements certified by individuals who have passed either the American CPA exam or the ACCA exams. The Big-Four accounting firms in Russia and the large Russian enterprises prefer to hire accountants who possess these credentials as well as those who have the CMA and/or CFM. Official recognition by the Russian government has become irrelevant.

REFERENCES

ACCA. 2003. Correspondence with the Association of Chartered Certified Accountants, dated November 5. Also www.accaglobal.com.

Anon. 2003a. The Plan for Transition towards IFRS is Approved by the Russian Government. *ICAR Newsletter* (January/February). http://www.icar.ru/eng/newsletter/0.2.2003.html.

Anon. 2003b. Russia to Implement IFRS – Starting in 2004. ICAR Newsletter (January/February). http://www.icar.ru/eng/newsletter/1.2.2003.html.

Anon. 2003c. BDO UNICONRUF and BDO International Present a Real Alternative to the "Big Four" in Russia and the World. *ICAR Newsletter* (January/February) http://www.icar.ru/eng/newsletter/11.2.2003.html.

Anon. 2003d. CIPA-EN Program is an Opportunity for Local Business to Develop and Integrate into the World Economy. *MIRROR*, Issue 8 (May) pp. 10-11. Quarterly newsletter of the USAID-Pragma Enterprise Development Project in Central Asia. www.casme.net.

Anon. 2003e. The First CAPS in Central Asia – The Impact of Accounting Reform. *MIRROR*, Issue 8 (May) pp. 3-4. Quarterly newsletter of the USAID-Pragma Enterprise Development Project in Central Asia. www.casme.net.

Anon. 2003f. CIPA Exams Taking Root. *MIRROR*, Issue 7 (February) p. 2. Quarterly newsletter of the USAID-Pragma Enterprise Development Project in Central Asia. www.casme.net.

Anon. 2001. Accountants in Russia Gain International Skills. Financial Management 44 (April).

Burnham, Lew. 2000. SRO Development Recommendations. *ICAR Newsletter* (December). www.icar.ru/eng/newsletter/3.12.2000.html.

CIA, Country Ranking website. www.countryrankings.com/rankorder/2119rank.html.

Enthoven, Adolf. 2003. Learning Accounting and Auditing in Russian. *Transition Newsletter*, World Bank (January, February, March) http://www.worldbank.org/transitionnewsletter/janfebmar03/boxpg22.htm.

Hong Kong, Census and Statistics Department http://www.info.gov.hk/censtatd/eng/hkstat/hkinf/population/pop1_index.html.

International Center for Accounting Reform. 2000. *Accounting Reform Recommendations*. Para. 4.13. Moscow. 28 September 2000. www.icar.ru/eng/report.zip.

International Center for Accounting Reform. 1999. Andrey Petrov: We Should Have One Profession. *ICAR Newsletter* (September), www.icar.ru/eng/newsletter/3.9.1999.html.

ICMA. 2003. Institute of Certified Management Accountants, correspondence November 5.

Johnson, Robert R. and Jan R. Squires. 2003. Forty Years and Going Strong: A Look at the Current State of the CFA Program. Association for Investment Management and Research. www.aimr.org/pdf/cfaprogram/CFAprogram.pdf.

McGee, Robert W. and Galina G. Preobragenskaya. 2004. Problems of Implementing International Accounting Standards in a Transition Economy: A Case Study of Russia. Presented at the Eighth International Conference on Global Business and Economic Development, Guadalajara, Mexico, January 7-10, 2004. http://papers.ssrn.com/sol3/papers.cfm?abstract_id=459363.

McGee, Robert W. 1999a. Certification of Accountants and Auditors in the CIS: A Case Study of Armenia. *Journal of Accounting, Ethics & Public Policy* 2(2): 338-353.

McGee, Robert W. 1999b. International Certification of Accountants in the CIS: A Case Study of Armenia. *Journal of Accounting, Ethics & Public Policy* 2(1): 70-75.

McGee, Robert W., Galina G. Preobragenskaya and Michael Tyler. 2004a. International Accounting Certification in the Russian Language: A Case Study. Presented at the International Academy of Business and Public Administration Disciplines (IABPAD) Conference, Tunica, Mississippi, May 24-26. http://ssrn.com/abstract=538622.

McGee, Robert W., Galina G. Preobragenskaya and Michael Tyler. 2004b. English Language International Accounting Certification in the CIS, Eastern and Central Europe. Presented at the International Academy of Business and Public Administration Disciplines (IABPAD) Conference, Tunica, Mississippi, May 24-26. http://ssrn.com/abstract=538602.

Prometric. www.prometric.com.

Rozhnova, Olga. 2000. The Problem of Perception of New Russian Accounting Standards. *ICAR Newsletter* (December). www.icar.ru/eng/newsletter/13/12/2000.html.

USAID-Pragma Enterprise Development Project in Central Asia website www.casme.net/docs/newPDFeng/AR_FINALAAA%20(3).pdf.

Zhuravlev, Igor. 2001. International Accounting Qualification: Is It Supplementary Education or Necessity. *ICAR Newsletter* (July/August) http://www.icar.ru/eng/newsletter/19.8.2001.html.

Chapter 9

CONCLUDING COMMENTS

The changes that have occurred in Russia's accounting and financial reporting system in recent years have been relatively rapid if one looks at it historically. Going from a centrally planned economy to a market economy in such a short period of time is something that has never been attempted before. There are no maps or guidelines that instruct government leaders how to do it (Shleifer and Treisman 2000). Yet Russia and the other countries that are transitioning from central planning to a market economy have all made good attempts to shift, with varying degrees of success.

Although much distance has been covered, much remains to be done. Fortunately for Russia, the market is rushing in to fill the void. Although Russia is in the process of adopting IFRS, adoption is far from complete. The Russian government has no present plans to adopt some of the IFRS and some of the standards that have already been adopted are not Cyrillic mirror images of the original standards that emanate out of London. But in a sense it doesn't matter. The Russian companies that most need to attract foreign capital are using the complete set of IFRS anyway. They are able to do it because they retain the services of accounting and consulting firms that are quite familiar with IFRS.

That has created some problems for Russian accounting and audit firms. The Big-Four accounting firms and a few smaller international accounting and consultancy firms are grabbing the lion's share of the business from the largest Russian enterprises because they are the only firms that have the expertise to provide the advice and services that the largest Russian enterprises require. They are more familiar with IFRS than are their Russian counterparts and they are able to read IFRS in the original English, which alleviates any problems that would arise from mediocre, incorrect or nonexistent translations. They also have a time advantage over their Russian counterparts because the Russian translation of newly issued IFRS is not available for several months after the English version has been issued.

There is still a widespread perception among the Russian accounting community that IFRS are not needed or relevant. This viewpoint retards the adoption and spread of IFRS. However, their view does have an element of truth to it. Many Russian firms and managers still view accounting as not much more than the collection of statistical information, which is prepared mostly for the tax authorities. This view is supported by the tax authorities themselves, who are not interested in reading financial statements that are prepared using IFRS.

This opinion about the lack of need for IFRS has had an effect on accounting education. If a large segment of the accounting profession does not see the relevance of IFRS, there is not much demand for offering or attending classes where practitioners can learn about IFRS. However, as Russian enterprises attempt to attract foreign capital, the demand for knowledge of IFRS will increase and this increased demand will be reflected in offering more classes and seminars on IFRS that will be attended by an increasing number of practitioners.

The teaching of IFRS has increased in Russian universities in recent years. This trend can be expected to continue. The lack of willing and qualified accounting professors will also be reduced with the passage of time, as IFRS become more widespread and as university students become university graduates, practitioners and teachers.

A two-tier structure has emerged as a result of the increased demand for financial statements that are prepared using IFRS or U.S. GAAP. The Big-Four accounting firms have a structural advantage over their Russian counterparts because they are able to read IFRS in the original English. These firms are also more familiar with IFRS because they have more experience using and applying IFRS. Furthermore, the Big-Four can draw on the vast supply of training materials that have been prepared by their various foreign offices. Russian accounting firms cannot draw on this wealth of accounting literature, which makes it more difficult for the Russian firms to train their own employees or clients. This structural advantage enjoyed by the Big-Four accounting firms will not dissipate in the foreseeable future. Thus, they will continue to be the preferred choice of the largest Russian enterprises for years to come. The smaller Russian firms will have to be content with servicing small and medium-size clients.

What has been said about IFRS might also be said about International Standards on Auditing (ISA). The Big-Four firms are more familiar with ISA than are their Russian counterparts, although that is changing. There is also the widespread perception that ISA audits are not needed, since Russian auditing standards have worked well for so many years. That may or may not be the case, but the perception exists. Of course, holding such a perception does not necessarily retard progress, especially in the case of the larger Russian enterprises, since they almost always retain the services of one of the Big-Four accounting firms, and all of these firms conduct ISA audits as a matter of course. So the fact that ISA are not always held in the highest regard by a substantial segment of the Russian audit community may not be a significant barrier to the transition process. The market process is at work to implement ISA where demand calls for it.

Corporate governance is still in its infancy in Russia. Even the largest enterprises do not have corporate governance policies that can compare to those of most companies in Western Europe and the United States. Things will change but it will take time. Russian directors feel uncomfortable with transparency and shareholder rights issues. They hesitate to grant rights to minority shareholders because they believe that doing so will weaken their own power and their grip on the enterprise. They resist appointing independent directors because they are independent. They prefer to appoint people they can control.

Russian companies have a difficult time attracting foreign investment, although the situation is not hopeless. Enterprises that publish financial statements based either on IFRS or U.S. GAAP are better able to attract capital.

Russia's tax system has improved greatly in the last few years. It used to be that the rules were obscure and contradictory and that rates were high. The rules have become less ambiguous over time and rates have dropped. Russia has instituted a flat tax, which is something the United States has not been able to do.

Accounting education in Russia has been going through rapid changes. A whole new generation of students is learning something about IFRS and ISA, although perhaps not enough. But it is a start. Accounting education is hampered by the fact that materials are still inadequate and good professors are hard to find at Russian university wages. But the situation is getting better.

National certification exists in Russia but those who pass the national certification exams are not as much in demand in the workplace as are those who can pass any of the several of the English language certification exams. Part of the problem is that some Russian certifications are for sale. Another reason for the lower prestige of Russian accounting certification is because of the perception that certification exams are more like university exams than true certification exams.

One disadvantage of the English language certification exams is that they service only a small minority of the market – those who can read English well enough to pass the exams. There is no Russian equivalent for these exams, although the CAP and CIPA exams are trying to provide a Russian alternative. As more people learn about the CAP and CIPA alternatives, and as more people take and pass their exams, perhaps these exams will be perceived as the equivalent of the English language counterparts. That is the goal of the CAP and CIPA programs. Offering exams like CAP and CIPA also have a positive influence on accounting education in Russia as well as in the other countries where they are offered, because they expose exam candidates to IFRS.

Much is happening in the area of accounting reform in Russia and the other former Soviet republics but much remains to be done. The other former Soviet countries are facing the same problems that accountants in Russia face – lack of demand for financial statements prepared using IFRS,, perceived lack of value of IFRS, lack of knowledge of IFRS by existing practitioners, mediocre translations, lack of study materials and lack of good accounting professors who are willing to work for low wages. Each country has its own story, although each story has some common elements. It would be interesting to see how closely the history of accounting reform in some of these other countries parallels the Russian experience.

Before 1989 all Soviet republics had the same accounting system. Since then, each former Soviet republic has been trying to adopt a market model by cutting its own path. Conducting comparative studies would be very enlightening. One could compare and contrast the various approaches and attempt to determine which approaches worked better and why.

One could also replicate the present study of accounting reform in Russia a few years down the road. Things are changing so rapidly that a follow-up study could yield some additional information, which would add to the literature as well as our understanding of economic reform.

Corporate governance is another area that is ripe for research. Russia is moving slowly in this area but some other former Soviet republics are moving even slower. It would be interesting to compare and contrast the corporate reform efforts in the various former Soviet republics and try to determine why they are moving at different rates of speed. Such studies could also perhaps give some insights as to why some approaches have been better than others.

Taxation and the public finance systems of the various former Soviet republics is also fertile ground for research. Some former republics, most notably Latvia and Estonia, have come a long way in terms of reforming their public finance systems. One might investigate how they were able to become so relatively successful while other former Soviet republics have lagged behind. One might also do comparative studies of one or more former Soviet republics, or one or more former Soviet republics might have their tax system compared to some countries in Eastern Europe, or to Western Europe or the OECD countries.

One might take a look at the former Soviet republics that have established low tax rates, such as Estonia and Latvia, and compare their tax systems to that of Ireland or some other EU country that has relatively low tax rates. Examining the similarities and differences could prove to be enlightening.

Studies could also be done of foreign direct investment and how various former Soviet republics have attempted to attract it. Some republics have been more successful than others in attracting foreign capital. It would be interesting to attempt to discover the reasons for the relative success of some countries or failure of others.

Studying accounting education in transition economies is another area ripe for investigation. Practically nothing has been done in this area until very recently. A study of one former Soviet republic could be done. Studies comparing the changes in accounting education in two or more former Soviet republics could also prove to be interesting. Comparative studies of Russian universities with those of some Western country could also be made.

Accounting education need not be limited to education at government universities. Many private universities have sprouted throughout Russia in the last few years. It would be interesting to see what they have done and are doing in the area of accounting education. It would also be interesting to compare various private universities to see if they are all basically the same or if there are substantial differences. It would also be interesting to see if some accounting education models have become more popular than others.

Another area of accounting education that has rarely been explored is accounting education of existing practitioners, or what might be called continuing professional education (CPE). Some former Soviet republics require a certain amount of CPE for license holders to maintain their accounting certification. Examining the growth of CPE courses in one or more countries would be interesting, as would comparative studies of CPE training in two or more former Soviet republics.

Further studies of accounting certification are also called for. The ACCA, CMA, CFM and other international certification exams are offered in countries other than Russia. Research could be done to see how English language certification is going in some other countries. If the results are mixed, or if results vary country to country, it would be interesting to try to determine the reasons for the differences.

Tracking the progress and evolution of the CAP and CIPA exams would also be interesting. These exams started just a few years ago, mostly in Central Asia. They have since started to spread to Russia, Ukraine and Moldova and could spread to some other Russian speaking countries.

Research on accounting and financial system reform in transition economies provides a wealth of opportunities for those who are interested in accounting research. It is a relatively new area where much work still needs to be done.

REFERENCES

Shleifer, Andrei and Daniel Treisman. 2000. *Without a Map: Political Tactics and Economic Reform in Russia*. Cambridge, MA and London: The MIT Press.

REFERENCES

Adams, Carol A. and Katarzyna M. McMillan, 1997. Internationalizing Financial Reporting in a Newly Emerging Market Economy: The Polish Example, *Advances in International Accounting* 10: 139-164.

Akhitirov, Artyam. 2003. Does Anyone Pay Taxes These Days? *Pravda.Ru.* November 19. http://english.pravda.ru/printed.html?news_id=11303

Albrecht, W. Steve & Robert J. Sack. 2002. *Accounting Education: Charting the Course through a Perilous Future.* Sarasota, FL: American Accounting Association www.aaahq.org/pubs/AESv16/toc.htm.

Alexander, David and Simon Archer. 2003. *Miller International Accounting Standards Guide.* New York: Aspen Law & Business.

An EYe on Russia, monthly newsletter published by the Ernst & Young Russia office [www.ey.com/global/content.nsf/Russia_E/Home].

Andersen, BDO, Deloitte Touche Tohmatsu, Ernst & Young, Grant Thornton, KPMG and PricewaterhouseCoopers. *GAAP 2001: A Survey of National Accounting Rules Benchmarked against International Accounting Standards.* The Russian Federation is covered at pp. 110-113. Available at [www.pwcglobal.com]

Anon. 2003. Russia's Richest Man Arrested on Fraud, Tax Evasion Charges. *Yahoo! News Asia.* October 26.
http://asia.news.yahoo.com/031025/afp/031025201623eco.html

Anon. 2003. Teaching in Russia, #2 (February),
www.ht/prof/rang/rang_prof.html

ACCA. 20 03. C orrespondence w ith t he As sociation o f C hartered C ertified Accountants, dated November 5. Also www.accaglobal.com.

Anon. 2003. The Plan for Transition towards IFRS is Approved by the Russian Government. *ICAR Newsletter* (January/February).
http://www.icar.ru/eng/newsletter/0.2.2003.html

Anon. 2003. Russia to Implement IFRS – Starting in 2004. ICAR Newsletter (January/February). http://www.icar.ru/eng/newsletter/1/2/2003.html

Anon. 2003. BDO UNICONRUF and BDO International Present a Real Alternative to the "Big Four" in Russia and the World. *ICAR Newsletter* (January/February) http://www.icar.ru/eng/newsletter/11.2.2003.html

Anon. 2003. CIPA-EN Program is an Opportunity for Local Business to Develop and Integrate into the World Economy. *MIRROR*, Issue 8 (May) pp. 10-11. Quarterly newsletter of the USAID-Pragma Enterprise Development Project in Central Asia. www.casme.net

Anon. 2003. The First CAPS in Central Asia – The Impact of Accounting Reform. *MIRROR*, Issue 8 (May) pp. 3-4. Quarterly newsletter of the USAID-Pragma Enterprise Development Project in Central Asia.
www.casme.net

Anon. 2003. CIPA Exams Taking Root. *MIRROR*, Issue 7 (February) p. 2. Quarterly newsletter of the USAID-Pragma Enterprise Development Project in Central Asia. www.casme.net

Anon. 2002. CIMA Supports Ongoing Russian Management Accounting Reform. *Financial Management* (July/August): 46.

Anon. 2002. Russia Heads for International Accounting Standards. *International Tax Review* 13:8 (September): 4.

Anon. 2001. Accountants in Russia Gain International Skills. *Financial Management* (April): 44.

Anon. 2001. Dirt Leaks Out. *Economist* July 7, p. 62.

Anon. 2001. Minority What? *Economist*, 358(8210), 72 (February 24).

Anon. 2001. Finance and Economics: Tax Beast. *The Economist* 358(8211): 71 (March 3).

Anon. (December 2000/January 2001). S&P Devises Scoring System for Corporate Governance Risk. *Central European* 10(10), 20-21.

Anon. 1998. Russia's Tax Revulsion. *The Christian Science Monitor*, March 12.

Anon. 1997. Russian Auditors Can Now Work to Unified Standards. *Current Digest of the Post Soviet Press*. 49:27, August 6, p. 12.

Anon. 1994. Tanya Bondarenko Seeks American Education. *Baylor Business Review* 12:1 (Spring): 12-15.

Arndt, H.W. 1987. *Economic Development: The History of an Idea*. Chicago: University of Chicago Press.

Arthur Andersen, BDO, Deloitte Touche Tohmatsu, Ernst & Young International, Grant Thornton, KPMG and PricewaterhouseCoopers. *GAAP 2000: A Survey of National Accounting Rules in 53 Countries*. The Russian Federation is covered at pp. 89-91. Available at [www.pwcglobal.com]

Bailey, Derek T. 1982. Accounting in Russia: The European Connection. *International Journal of Accounting* 18(1), 1-36.

Baker, Stephanie. 1998. Russia: Tax Chief Targets Rich and Famous. *Radio Free Europe*, Radio Liberty, June 5. www.rferl.org/nca/features/1998/06/F.RU.98060152350.html

Bauer, Peter. 1991. *The Development Frontier: Essays in Applied Economics*. Cambridge, MA: Harvard University Press.

Bauer, Peter. 1976. *Dissent on Development*, revised edition. Cambridge, MA: Harvard University Press.

BDO, Deloitte Touche Tohmatsu, Ernst & Young, Grant Thornton, KPMG and PricewaterhouseCoopers. *GAAP Convergence 2002: A Survey of National Efforts to Promote and Achieve Convergence with International Financial Reporting Standards*. Available at [www.pwcglobal.com]

Bird, Richard M. 1992. *Tax Policy & Economic Development*. Baltimore and London: The Johns Hopkins University Press.

Black, B. 2001. Does Corporate Governance Matter? A Crude Test Using Russian Data, *University of Pennsylvania Law Review* 149(6), 2131-2150 (June).

Blum, Walter J. and Harry Kalven, Jr. 1953. *The Uneasy Case for Progressive Taxation.* Chicago: University of Chicago Press.

Borda, Maria and Stuart McLeay, 1996. Accounting and Economic Transformation in Hungary, in Neil Garrod and Stuart McLeay, editors, *Accounting in Transition: The Implications of Political and Economic Reform in Central Europe,* London and New York: Routledge 116-140.

Boross, Z., A.H. Clarkson, M. Fraser and P. Weetman, 1995. Pressures and Conflicts in Moving towards Harmonization of Accounting Practice: the H ungarian E xperience, *T he European Accounting Review* 4(4): 713-737.

Breton, Albert. 1998. *Competitive Governments: An Economic Theory of Politics and Public Finance.* Cambridge, UK and New York: Cambridge University Press.

British Accounting Association Corporate Governance Special Interest Group website www.baacgsig.qub.ac.uk/

Buchanan, James M. 1967. *Public Finance in Democratic Process.* Chapel Hill: University of North Carolina Press.

Buchanan, James M. and Marilyn R. Flowers. 1975. *The Public Finances,* 4th edition. Homewood, IL: Richard D. Irwin, Inc.

Buck, T. 2003. Modern Russian Corporate Governance: Convergent Forces or Product of Russia's History? *Journal of World Business,* 38(4), 299-313.

Burnham, Lew. 2000. SRO Development Recommendations. *ICAR Newsletter* (December). www.icar.ru/eng/newsletter/3.12.2000.html

Burns, Stuart. 1999. Original Sin. *Accountancy,* October, p. 42.

Bychkova, Svetlana. 1996. The Development and Status of Auditing in Russia. *The European Accounting Review* 5:1, 77-90.

Bychkova, Svetlana and Natalya Lebedeva. 2001. Comparing the Russian Auditing Regulations against Western Standards. *Accounting Report* (ICAR) (January/February): 24-28. [www.icar.ru]

Cadbury, A., et al. 1992. (The Cadbury Report) *Report of the Committee on Financial Aspects of Corporate Governance* (December 1), London: Gee Publishing Ltd... Available at
www.worldbank.org/html/fpd/privatesector/cg/docs/cadbury.pdf

Campbell, Robert W. 1963. *Accounting in Soviet Planning and Management.* Russian Research Center Series 45, Cambridge, Harvard University Press.

Campbell, Robert W. 1956. Accounting for Depreciation in the Soviet Economy. *Quarterly Journal of Economics* 70(4), 481-506.

Chan, M.W. Luke and Wendy Rotenberg, 1999. Accounting, Accounting Education, and Economic Reform in the People's Republic of China, *International Studies of Management & Organization* 29(3): 37-53.

Chastain, C.E. 1982. Soviet Accounting Lags Behind the Needs of Enterprise Managers. *Management International Review* 22(4), 12-18.

Chazan, Guy and Jeanne Whalen. 2002. Russia to Probe Pricewaterhouse's Audits of Gazprom. *Wall Street Journal*, February 20, p. A16.

Cheney, Glenn Alan. 1990. Western Accounting Arrives in Eastern Europe. *Journal of Accountancy* (September): 40-43.

Choi, Frederick D.S., Carol Ann Frost and Gary K. Meek, 2002. *International Accounting*, fourth edition, Upper Saddle River, NJ: Prentice Hall.

CIA, Country Ranking website.
www.countryrankings.com/rankorder/2119rank.html

The Code of Professional Conduct of Independent Directors. 2003. Independent Director (newsletter), Spring, p. 11. [www.nand.ru]

Collingwood, H. 1991. The Soviets Take Accounting 101. *Business Week*, April 22, p.38.

Cornish, Keith. 1999. Taking IASs to Russia. *Accountancy* 124: 1271 (July): 54.

Corporate Governance Code, Russian Institute of Directors
www.rid.ru/db.php?db_id=516&1=en

Corporate Monitoring www.corpmon.com/

Coyle, William H. and Vladimir V. Platonov, 1998. Insights Gained from International Exchange and Educational Initiatives between Universities: The Challenges of Analyzing Russian Financial Statements, *Issues in Accounting Education* (February) 13(1): 223-233.

Crallan, Jocelyne, 1997. Accounting Reform in the CIS, *Management Accounting* (January) 34.

Cullis, John and Philip Jones. 1998. *Public Finance and Public Choice*. New York: Oxford University Press.

Currie, Antony. 1996. The Figures Behind the Figures. *Euromoney*, Issue 330, October, pp. 89-91.

Damant, David. 1999. IASs and the Capital Markets. *Accountancy: International Edition*, Vol. 123, No. 1269 (May), p. 80.

Danilevsky, Yuri, Oleg Ostrovsky and Eugeny Guttsait. 2001. Russian Audit Standards: Past, Present and Future. *Accounting Report* (ICAR) (January/February): 1, 9-11. [www.icar.ru]

Davis Global Advisors. *Leading Corporate Governance Indicators,* Newton, MA: Davis Global Advisors. Annual publication.
www.davisglobal.com/publications/lcgi/index.html

De Jouvenel, Bertrand. 1952; 1990. *The Ethics of Redistribution*. Cambridge, UK: Cambridge University Press (1952); Indianapolis: Liberty Press, 1990).

Easter, Gerald M. 2003. Building State Capacity in Post-Communist Russia: Tax Collection. www.ilpp.ru/projects/govern/pdf/Easter_full.pdf

Easter, Gerald M. 2002. Politics of Revenue Extraction in Post-Communist States: Poland and Russia Compared. *Politics & Society* 30(4): 599-627.

Encyclopedia of Corporate Governance www.encycogov.com/

Enthoven, Adolf J.H., Yaroslav V. Sokolov, Svetlana M. Bychkova, Valery V. Kovalev & Maria V. Semenova. 1998. *Accounting, Auditing and Taxation in the Russian Federation*. Montvale, NJ: Institute of Management Accountants & The Center for International Accounting Development, The University of Texas at Dallas.

Enthoven, Ado lf J.H., J aroslav V . S okolov a nd Al exander M . P etrachkov. 1992. *Doing Business in Russia and the Other Former Soviet Republics: Accounting and Joint Venture Issues*. Montvale, NJ: Institute of Management Accountants.

Enthoven, Adolf. 2003. Learning Accounting and Auditing in Russian. *Transition Newsletter*, World Bank (January, February, March) www.worldbank.org/transitionnewsletter/janfebmar03/boxpg22.htm

Enthoven, Adolf J.H., 1999. Russia's Accounting Moves West, *Strategic Finance* 81(1): 32-37.

Enthoven, Adolf J.H., 1992. Accounting in Russia: From Perestroika to Profits, *Management Accounting* 74(4): 27-31.

Epstein, Barry J. and Abbas Ali Mirza. 2003. *IAS 2003: Interpretation and Application of International Accounting Standards*. New York: John Wiley & Sons.

Ermakova, Tatiana. 2003. Tax Authorities Clarify Issues Regarding the Application of Chapter 25 of the Tax Code. *Legislative News*, July, pp. 1-5 [www.deloitte.ru].

Ernst & Young. 2002. *Tax Tables 2003 Russia*. www.ey.com

European Corporate Governance Institute website www.ecgi.org/

European Corporate Governance Institute link to Codes www.ecgi.org/codes/all_codes.htm

Feinberg, P. 2000. Historically Indifferent Russia Starts to Heed Corporate Governance Rules, *Pensions & Investments*, 28(23), 18-19 (November 13).

Figes, Orlando. 2002. *Natasha's Dance: A Cultural History of Russia*. New York: Henry Holt and Company.

Filatotchev, I., Buck, T. and Zhukov, V. 2000. Downsizing in Privatized Firms in Russia, Ukraine, and Belarus. *Academy of Management Journal*, 43(3), 286-304.

Filatotchev, I., Wright, M., Uhlenbruck, K., Tihanyi, L., and Hoskisson, R. 2003. Governance, Organizational Capabilities, and Restructuring in Transition Economies. *Journal of World Business*, 38(4), 331-347.

Forbes, Steve. 2003. Where Communists Beat Capitalists. *Forbes* 172(2): 16, July 21.

Friedman, Milton & Rose D. Friedman. 1984. *Tyranny of the Status Quo.* New York: Harcourt Brace Jovanovich.

GAAP Convergence 2002: A Survey of National Efforts to Promote and Achieve Convergence with International Financial Reporting Standards. 2002. BDO, Deloitte Touche Tohmatsu, Ernst & Young, Grant Thornton, KPMG & PricewaterhouseCoopers. Researched by Donna L. Street. [www.pwcglobal.com]

GAAP 2001: A Survey of National Accounting Rules Benchmarked against International Accounting Standards. 2001. A joint publication of Andersen, BDO, Deloitte Touche Tohmatsu, Ernst & Young, Grant Thornton, KPMG and PricewaterhouseCoopers, edited by Christopher W. Nobes. [www.kpmg.ru] [www.ifad.net]

GAAP 2000: A Survey of National Accounting Rules in 53 Countries. 2000. A joint publication of Arthur Andersen, BDO, Deloitte Touche Tohmatsu, Ernst & Young International, Grant Thornton, KPMG and PricewaterhouseCoopers, edited by Christopher W. Nobes. [www.pwcglobal.com]

Gabbin, Alexander L. 2002. The Crisis in Accounting Education. *Journal of Accountancy*, April, pp. 81-86.

Garrod, Neil & Stuart McLeay (Eds.). 1996. *Accounting in Transition: The Implications of Political and Economic Reform in Central Europe.* London & New York: Routledge.

Global Corporate Governance Forum www.gcgf.org/

Gorelik, George. 1974a. Notes on the Development and Problems of Soviet Uniform Accounting. *International Journal of Accounting* 9(2), 135-148.

Gorelik, George. 1974b. Soviet Accounting, Planning and Control. *Abacus* 10(1), 13-25.

Gorelik, George. 1971. Enterprise Profit and Profitability Measurements: Soviet-American Convergence. *International Journal of Accounting* 6(2), 1-14.

Greenbury, R. et al. 1995. (Greenbury Report). *Directors' Remuneration: Report of a Study Group Chaired by Sir Richard Greenbury*, (July 17), London: Gee Publishing Ltd. Available at www.baacgsig.qub.ac.uk/

Haigh, Art. 2001. We View Russia's Future with Optimism. *Kommersant-Daily*, January 26 [www.pwcglobal.ru/].

Hall, Robert E. and Alvin Rabushka. 1985. *The Flat Tax.* Stanford: Hoover Institution Press.

Hampel Committee. 1998. *Hampel Committee Report*, (January), London: Gee Publishing Ltd. Available at www.ecgi.org/codes/country_documents/uk/hampel_index.htm

Hanke, Steve H. and Alan A. Walters, editors. 1991. *Capital Markets and Development.* San Francisco: ICS Press.

Hayek, Friedrich A. (ed.) 1935. *Collectivist Economic Planning: Critical Studies on the Possibilities of Socialism*, London: George Routledge & Sons, Ltd., reprinted by Augustus M. Kelley Publishers, Clifton, NJ, 1975.

Heritage Foundation and Wall Street Journal. 2002. *2003 Index of Economic Freedom* [www.heritage.org/research/features/index/2003/index.html]

Hoff, Trygve J.B. 1981. *Economic Calculation in the Socialist Society.* Indianapolis: Liberty Press.

Hong Kong, Census and Statistics Department www.info.gov.hk/censtatd/eng/hkstat/hkinf/population/pop1_index.html

Horwitz, Bertrand. 1970. Accounting Controls and the Soviet Economic Reforms. *California Management Review* 13(1), 75-83.

Horwitz, Bertrand. 1963. Depreciation and Cost Stability in Soviet Accounting. *Accounting Review* 38(4), 819-826.

IASC (International Accounting Standards Committee). 1989. *Framework for the Preparation and Presentation of Financial Statements.* London: IASC.

ICAR (International Center for Accounting Reform). 2001. Recommendations for Accounting Reform in the CIS Countries. *ICAR Newsletter*, May/June. [www.icar.ru/eng/newsletter/22/6/2001.html]

ICAR. 2001. Poor Compliance and Poor Auditing Undermines Achievements on International Accounting Standards. *ICAR Newsletter*, March/April [www.icar.ru/eng/newsletter/4.4.2001.html]

ICAR. 2001. EU Takes Important Step in Support of Russia's Auditing Reform. *International Center for Accounting Reform Newsletter* March/April. [www.icar.ru/eng/newsletter/15.4.2001.html]

ICAR. 2000. Communique of the Thirteenth Session of the Foreign Investment Advisory Council in Russia. *International Center for Accounting Reform Newsletter.* November/December. [www.icar.ru/eng/newsletter/2.12.2000.html]

ICAR. 2000. ERBD Calls for Use of IAS. *International Center for Accounting Reform Newsletter,* November/December. [www.icar.ru/eng/newsletter/4.12.2000.html]

ICAR. 2000. *Accounting Reform Recommendations*, Moscow: International Center for Accounting Reform [www.icar.ru].

ICAR. 1999. Andrey Petrov: We Should Have One Profession. *ICAR Newsletter* (September) www.icar.ru/eng/newsletter/3.9.1999.html

ICAR Newsletter [www.icar.ru/] various issues.

Ichizli, Svetlana M. & Nicholas M. Zacchea. 2000. Accounting Reform in the Former Soviet Republics: An Essential Ingredient for Economic Independence. *Government Accountants Journal* 49(2), 46-53.

ICMA. 2003. Institute of Certified Management Accountants, correspondence November 5.

The Independent Directors Association Charter. 2003. *Independent Director*, Spring, p.12. [www.nand.ru].

Independent Directors Association website www.independentdirector.ru

Independent Directors Association. 2003. *Independent Director Code* (April 15 Draft), Moscow: Independent Directors Association. Available at www.independentdirector.ru

Index of Economic Freedom. 2003. New York: The Wall Street Journal and Washington, DC: The Heritage Foundation [www.heritage.org/research/features/index/]

Institute of Corporate Law and Corporate Governance website www.iclg.ru

Institute of Corporate Law and Corporate Governance. 2002. *Managing Corporate Governance Risks in Russia* (May), Moscow: Institute of Corporate Law and Corporate Governance.

International Center for Accounting Reform (ICAR). 2000. *Accounting Reform Recommendations* [www.icar.ru/eng/report.zip]

International Center for Accounting Reform (ICAR). 2000. The Accounting Reform Recommendations. *Accounting Report* (ICAR), October 3, 2000 [www.icar.ru/eng/newsletter/3.10.2000.html]

International C enter for A ccounting R eform (ICAR). 1999. *C onsiderations concerning the establishment of accounting standards in the Russian Federation*, September.

International Corporate Governance Network website www.icgn.org/

International Federation of Accountants, 2001. Strategy for Implementation of IFAC International Education Guideline No. 9: "Prequalification Education, Tests of Professional Competence and Practical Experience of Professional Accountants:" A T ask Force Report of The International Association for Accounting Education and Research (IAAER), (February), New York: International Federation of Accountants, available at www.ifac.org

International Federation of Accountants, 2000. Assistance Projects in Accountancy Education and Development, A Study Based on the Experience of IFAC Member Bodies, Study Paper (February), New York: International Federation of Accountants, available at www.ifac.org

International Finance Corporation, Russia Corporate Governance Project website www2.ifc.org/rcgp/English.htm

Iskyan, K. 2002. Clean-up Time in Russia, *Global Finance* 32-35 (February).

Jaruga, Alicja. 1996. Accounting in Socialist Countries: The Beginnings of Reform. In Neil Garrod & Stuart McLeay (eds.), *Accounting in Transition: The Implications of Political and Economic Reform in Central Europe* (pp. 12-27). London & New York: Routledge.

Jermakowicz, Eva and Dolores F. Rinke, 1996. The New Accounting Standards in the Czech Republic, Hungary, and Poland vis-à-vis International Accounting Standards and European Union Directives, *Journal of International Accounting Auditing & Taxation* 5(1): 73-88.

Johnson, Robert R. and Jan R. Squires. 2003. Forty Years and Going Strong: A Look at the Current State of the CFA Program. Association for Investment Management and Research. www.aimr.org/pdf/cfaprogram/CFAprogram.pdf

Judge, W.Q., Naoumova, I. & Kutzevol, N. 2003. *Corporate Governance in Russia: An Empirical Study of Russian Managers' Perception*. Paper presented at the Gorbachev Foundation Conference on Corporate Governance in Transition Economies held at Northeastern University, Boston, April 2003. Published in *Journal of World Business*, 38(4), 385-396 (November 2003) under the title Corporate Governance and Firm Performance in Russia: An Empirical Study.

Kemp, Peter and David Alexander, 1996. Accountancy and Financial Infrastructure in Central and Eastern European Countries, *European Business Journal* 8(4): 14-21.

King, N., A. Beattie and A.-M. Cristescu, 2001. Developing Accounting and Audit in a Transition Economy: The Romanian Experience, *The European Accounting Review* 10(1): 149-171.

Klebnikov, Paul. 2001. A Putin Play. *Forbes* 168:8 (October 1): 128.

Kobrack, F. & G. Feldman. 1991. Is There an Accounting Textbook Market in the Soviet Union? *Publishers Weekly*, September 20, pp. 43-44.

KPMG 2003. *Doing Business in Russia*. July [www.kpmg.ru].

KPMG. *Russia – Tax Overview* [www.kpmg.ru].

Krzywda, Danuta, Derek Bailey and Marek Schroeder, 1996. The Impact of Accounting Regulation on Financial Reporting in Poland, in Neil Garrod and Stuart McLeay, editors, *Accounting in Transition: The Implications of Political and Economic Reform in Central Europe*, London and New York: Routledge 61-92.

Krzywda, Danuta, Derek Bailey and Marek Schroeder, 1995. A Theory of European Accounting Development Applied to Accounting Change in Contemporary Poland, *The European Accounting Review* 4(4): 625-657.

Kulikova, Lidia I. 1999. *Financial Accounting*, Kazan, Russia, second edition.

Lal, Deepak. 2001. *Unintended Consequences: The Impact of Factor Endowments, Culture and Politics on Long-Term Economic Performance.* Cambridge, MA: MIT Press.

Lal, Deepak. 1986. *The Poverty of Development Economics*. Cambridge, MA: Harvard University Press.

Lange, Oskar. 1937. On the Economic Theory of Socialism, I I, *Review of Economic Studies* 4(2), 123-42.

Lange, Oskar. 1936. On the Economic Theory of Socialism, I. *Review of Economic Studies* 4(1), 53-71.

Larson, Robert K. and Sara York. 1996. Accounting Standard-Setting Strategies and Theories of Economic Development: Implications for the Adoption of International Accounting Standards. *Advances in International Accounting,* Vol. 9, pp. 1-20.

Larson, Robert K. 1993. International Accounting Standards and Economic Growth: An Empirical Investigation of Their Relationship in Africa. *Research in Third World Accounting*, Vol. 2, pp. 27-43.

Law on Education, 10 July 1992, #3266-1.

Law on High and Post-university Education, 22 August 1996, #125 FZ.

Lebow, Marc I. & Rasoul H. Tondkar. 1986. Accounting in the Soviet Union. *International Journal of Accounting* 22(1), 61-79.

Legislative Tracking, Deloitte & Touche newsletter [www.deloitte.ru].

Lerner, Abba P. 1935. Economic Theory and Socialist Economy. *Review of Economic Studies* 2, 51-61.

Lihachev, V.N. 1918. *30 Lessons in Double Entry Bookkeeping*, Moscow: K.I. Tihimirov's Trade House, fourth edition.

Lin, Z hijun a nd S hengliang D eng, 1992. E ducating Accountants i n C hina: Current Experiences and Future Prospects, *International Journal of Accounting* 27(2): 164-77.

Lindberg, Deborah L. 2002. The Use of Barter Hampers Implementation of International Accounting Standards and Contributes to Financial Woes in the Russian Federation. *Russian & East European Finance and Trade* 38:3 (May/June): 5-17.

Lippincott, Benjamin E. (Ed.). 1938. *On the Economic Theory of Socialism*. Minneapolis: University of Minnesota Press.

Mackevicius, Jonas, Juozas Aliukonis and Derek Bailey, 1996. The Reconstruction of National Accounting Rules in Lithuania, in Neil Garrod and S tuart M cLeay, e ditors, *Ac counting in Transition: The Implications of Political and Economic Reform in Central Europe*, London and New York: Routledge 43-60.

McCaffery, Edward J. 2002. *Fair Not Flat: How to Make the Tax System Better and Simpler*. Chicago: University of Chicago Press.

McCarthy, D.J. and Puffer, S.M. 2003. Corporate Governance in Russia: A Framework for Analysis. *Journal of World Business*, 38(4), 397-415.

McCarthy, D.J. and Puffer, S.M. 2002. Corporate Governance in Russia: Towards a European, US, or Russian Model? *European Management Journal*, 20(6), 630-641.

McGee, Robert W. 2004. *The Philosophy of Taxation and Public Finance.* Dordrecht, London and Boston: Kluwer Academic Publishers.

McGee, Robert W. 2003. Educating Professors in a Transition Economy: A Case Study of Bosnia & Herzegovina. Proceedings of the Twelfth World Business Congress, International Management Development Association, Vancouver, BC, Canada, June 25-29, 2003, pp. 155-162. Available at [www.ssrn.com].

McGee, Robert W. 2003. Reforming Accounting Education in a Transition Economy: A Case Study of Armenia. Proceedings of the Twelfth World Business Congress, International Management Development Association, Vancouver, BC, Canada, June 25-29, 2003, pp. 139-146. Available at [www.ssrn.com].

McGee, Robert W. 1999. Why People Evade Taxes in Armenia: A Look at an Ethical Issue Based on a Summary of Interviews. *Journal of Accounting, Ethics & Public Policy* 2(2): 408-416.

McGee, Robert W. 1993. Principles of Taxation for Emerging Economies: Lessons from the U.S. Experience. *Dickinson Journal of International Law* 12: 29-93.

McGee, Robert W. 1999.The Problem of Implementing International Accounting Standards: A Case Study of Armenia, *Journal of Accounting, Ethics & Public Policy* 2(1): 38-41. Also available at WWW.SSRN.COM

McGee, Robert W. 1999. Certification of Accountants and Auditors in the CIS: A Case Study of Armenia, *Journal of Accounting, Ethics & Public Policy* 2(2): 338-353. Also available at WWW.SSRN.COM

McGee, Robert W., Galina G. Preobragenskaya and Michael Tyler. 2004. International Accounting Certification in t he Russian Language: A Case Study. Presented at the International Academy of Business and Public Administration Disciplines (IABPAD) Conference, Tunica, Mississippi, May 24-26. WWW.SSRN.COM

McGee, Robert W., Galina G. Preobragenskaya and Michael Tyler. 2004. English Language International Accounting Certification in the CIS, Eastern and Central Europe. Presented at the International Academy of Business and Public Administration Disciplines (IABPAD) Conference, Tunica, Mississippi, May 24-26. WWW.SSRN.COM

McGee, Robert W. and Galina G. Preobragenskaya. 2004. Problems of Implementing International Accounting Standards in a Transition Economy: A Case Study of Russia. Presented at the Eighth International Conference on Global Business and Economic Development, Guadalajara, Mexico, January 7-10, 2004. WWW.SSRN.COM

Metzger, B., Dean, R.N. and Bloom, D. 2002. Russia's Code of Corporate Conduct: An Innovative Approach to Solving Shareholder Rights

Abuses, *The Corporate Governance Advisor*10 (2), 12-17 (March/April).

Miller, S. 2002. L aw a nd O rder M akes its M ark, *Banker* 152(913), 44- 45 (March).

Mills, Robert H. & Abbott L. Brown. 1966. Soviet Economic Development and Accounting. *Journal of Accountancy* 121(6), 40-46.

Mises, Ludwig von. 1935. Economic Calculation in the Socialist Commonwealth. In Friedrich A. Hayek (Ed.), *Collectivist Economic Planning: Critical Studies on the Possibilities of Socialism* (pp. 87-130) London: George Routledge & Sons, Ltd., reprinted by Augustus M. Kelley Publishers, Clifton, NJ, 1975.

Mises, Ludwig von. 1923. Neue Beitrage zum Problem der sozialistischen Wirtschaftsrechnung [New Contributions to the Problem of Socialist Economic Calculation], *Archiv fur Sozialwissenschaft und Sozial Politik* 51, December, pp. 488-500.

Mises, Ludwig von. 1922. *Die Gemeinwirtschaft*. The second German edition (1932) was translated into English by J. Kahane and published as *Socialism: An Economic and Sociological Analysis* by Jonathan Cape, London, 1936.

Mises, Ludwig von. 1920. Die Wirtschaftsrechnung im Sozialistischen Gemeinwesen [Economic Calculation in the Socialist Commonwealth]. *Archiv fur Sozialwissenschaft und Sozialpolitik* 47, 86-121.

Monks, R. A.G. & Minow, N. (Eds) 2004. *Corporate Go vernance*, third edition, London: Blackwell Publishers.

Motyka, Wolodymyr. 1990. The Impact of Western Europe on Accounting Development in Tsarist Russia Prior to 1800. *Abacus* 26(1), 36-62.

Muravyev, A. 2001. Turnover of Top Executives in Russian Companies. *Russian Economic Trends*, 10(1), 20-24.

Musgrave, Richard A. 1959. *The Theory of Public Finance: A Study in Public Economy*. New York, London and Toronto: McGraw-Hill Book Company.

Musgrave, Richard A. and Peggy B. Musgrave. 1976. *Public F inance in Theory and Practice*, 2nd edition. New York: McGraw-Hill Book Company.

Myre, Greg. 1996. In Russia, Tax Police Take New Approach to Cash Crisis. *Associated Press*, December 6. www.lubbockonline.com/news/120696/inrussia.htm

National Association of Corporate Directors website www.nacdonline.org/

Organisation for Economic Cooperation and Development website www.oecd.org

Organisation for Economic Cooperation and Development. 2003. *White Paper o n C orporate Go vernance in S outh Eas tern Eu rope*, Paris: OECD. www.oecd.org

Organisation for Economic Cooperation and Development. 2003. *Survey of Corporate Governance Developments in OECD Countries*, Paris: OECD.

Organisation for Economic Cooperation and Development. 2002. *White Paper on Corporate Governance in Russia*, (April 15), Paris: OECD. Available at www.oecd.org/dataoecd/47/50/4347646.pdf

Organisation for Economic Cooperation and Development. 1999. *Principles of Corporate Governance*, Paris: OECD. Available at www.oecd.org/dataoecd/47/50/4347646.pdf

Paliy, Vitaly. 2000. New Chart of Accounts Approved. *Accounting Report* (ICAR), December. [www.icar.ru]

Pankov, Dmitri, 1998. Accounting for Change in Belarus, *Management Accounting* (London) 76(10): 56-58.

Peng, M., Buck, T. and Filatotchev, I. 2003. Do Outside Directors and New Managers Help Improve Firm Performance? An Exploratory Study in Russian Privatization. *Journal of World Business*, 38(4), 348-360.

Pistor, K., Raiser, M. and Gelfer, S. 2000. Law and Finance in Transition Economies, *Economics of Transition* 8(2), 325-368.

Polanyi, Karl. 1923. Sozialistiche Rechnungslegung [Socialistic Accounting], *Archiv fur Sozialwissenschaft und Sozialpolitik* 49, 377-420.

Preobragenskaya, Galina G. and Robert W. McGee. 2004. Private Sector Accounting Education in Russia. Presented at the International Academy of Business and Public Administration Disciplines (IABPAD) Annual Conference, New Orleans, January 23-25. Available at WWW.SSRN.COM

Preobragenskaya, Galina G. and Robert W. McGee. 2004. International Accounting and Finance Certification in the Russian Federation. Presented at the 16th Annual Conference of the International Academy of Business Disciplines, San Antonio, Texas, March 25-28. Available at WWW.SSRN.COM

Preobragenskaya, Galina G. and Robert W. McGee. 2004. Recent Developments in Private Sector Accounting Education in Russia. Presented at the 16th Annual Conference of the International Academy of Business Disciplines, San Antonio, Texas, March 25-28. Available at WWW.SSRN.COM

Preobragenskaya, Galina G. & Robert W. McGee. 2003. International Accounting Standards and Foreign Direct Investment in Russia. Presented at the International Trade and Finance Association's Thirteenth International Conference, Vaasa, Finland, May 28-31, 2003. [www.ssrn.com]

Preobragenskaya, Galina G. & Robert W. McGee. 2003. The Current State of Auditing in Russia. In Jerry Biberman & Abbass F. Alkhafaji (Eds.), *Business Research Yearbook: Global Business Perspectives*, Volume X (pp.499-503) Saline, MI: McNaughton & Gunn, Inc. A longer version of this paper is posted at [www.ssrn.com].

PricewaterhouseCoopers. 2003. *Doing Business in the Russian Federation.* [www.pwcglobal.com/ru].

Prometric. www.prometric.com

Puffer, S.M. and McCarthy, D.J. 2003. The Emergence of Corporate Governance in Russia. *Journal of World Business*, 38(4), 284-298.

Rabushka, Alvin. 2002. Tax Reform Remains High on Russia's Policy Agenda. Hoover Institution Public Policy Inquiry. May 22. www.russianeconomy.org/comments/052202.html

Rabushka, Alvin. 2002. Improving Russia's 13% Flat Tax. Hoover Institution Public Policy Inquiry. March 11. www.russianeconomy.org/comments/031102.html

Rabushka, Alvin. 2002. The Flat Tax at Work in Russia. Hoover Institution Public Policy Inquiry. February 21. www.russianeconomy.org/comments/022102.html

Rabushka, Alvin and Pauline Ryan. 1982. *The Tax Revolt.* Stanford: Hoover Institution Press.

Radoutsky, Alexander. 2001. Transparent Financial Information as a Factor of Economic Stability and Intensive Growth. *Accounting Report* (ICAR) (March/April): 18-19. [www.icar.ru/eng/newsletter/pdf/4.2001.pdf]

Ramcharran, Harri. 2000. The Need for International Accounting Harmonization: An Examination and Comparison of the Practices of Russian Banks. *American Business Review* 18:1 (January) 1-8.

Remizov, Nikolai. 2001. Issues of ISA Implementation in Russia. *Accounting Report* (ICAR) (January/February): 22-24. [www.icar.ru]

Richard, Jacques. 1998. Accounting in Eastern Europe: From Communism to Capitalism. In Peter Walton, Axel Haller & Bernard Raffournier (Eds.), *International Accounting* (pp. 295-323). London: International Thomson Business Press.

Roberts, Alan, 2001. The Recent Romanian Accounting Reforms: Another Case of Cultural Intrusion? in Yelena Kalyuzhnova and Michael Taylor, editors, *Transitional Economies: Banking, Finance, Institutions*, Basingstoke, UK and New York: Palgrave 146-166.

Robertson, C.J., Gilley, K.M., and Street, M.D. 2003. The Relationship between Ethics and Firm Practices in Russia and the United States. *Journal of World Business*, 38(4), 375-384.

Rolfe, Robert J. and Timothy S. Doupnik, 1995. Accounting Revolution in East Central Europe, *Advances in International Accounting* 8: 223-246.

Roth, K. and Kostova, T. 2003. Organizational Coping with Institutional Upheaval in Transition Economies. *Journal of World Business*, 38(4), 314-330.

Rothbard, Murray N. 1991. The End of Socialism and the Calculation Debate Revisited. *Review of Austrian Economics* 5(2), 51-76.

Rozhnova, Olga. 2000. The Problem of Perception of New Russian Accounting Standards. *Accounting Report* (ICAR), December 13, 2000 [www.icar.ru/eng/newsletter/13.12.2000.html]

Russia – Legislative News, Deloitte & Touche newsletter [www.deloitte.ru].

Russian Federation. 1998. Programme for the Reformation of Accounting in Accordance with IAS. Decision of Government of Russian Federation #283, March 6.

Russian Legislation website, Ernst & Young [www.tax.eycis.com].

Russian Corporate Governance Roundtable website www.corp-gov.org/

Russian Institute of Directors website www.rid.ru

Russian Institute of Directors. 2003. *Structure and Activities of Boards of Directors of Russian Joint-Stock Companies.* Moscow: Russian Institute of Directors. www.rid.ru

Russian Institute of Directors. 2002. *Corporate Governance Code* (April 5), Moscow: Russian Institute of Directors www.rid.ru

Schneidman, Leonid. 2003. "The Long Road to IAS." *Kommersant*, June 9 [www.pwcglobal.com/ru].

Scott, George M. 1969. Accounting and Economic Reform in the Soviet Union. *Abacus* 5(1), 55-63.

Seal, Willie, Pat Sucher and Ivan Zelenka, 1995. The Changing Organization of Czech Accounting, *The European Accounting Review* 4(4): 659-681.

Sennholz, Hans. 2002. Russia's March from Communism. September 12, Auburn, AL: Mises Institute. [www.mises.org].

Shama, Avraham & Christopher G. McMahan. 1990. Perestroika and Soviet Accounting: From a Planned to a Market Economy. *International Journal of Accounting* 25(3), 155-168.

Shatalov, S. 2003. Russian Standards Approach IFRS. *Prime-TASS*. Business type. 01.23.03.

Shaw, Sue Olinger, Nina Burakova and Valery Makoukha. 2000. Economic Education in Russia: A Case Study. *S.A.M. Advanced Management Journal* 65:3 (Summer): 29-34.

Shleifer, Andrei and Daniel Treisman. 2000. Without a Map: Political Tactics and Economic Reform in Russia. Cambridge and London: The MIT Press.

Shneydman, L. 2002. Introduction of IAS in Russia. *ICAR Newsletter*, April 1 [www.icar.ru/rus/newsletter/1/4/2002]

Smirnova, Irina A., Jaroslav V. Sokolov and Clive R. Emmanuel, 1995. Accounting Education in R ussia T oday, *The European Accounting Review* 4(4): 833-846.

Street, Donna L. 2002. GAAP 2001 – Benchmarking National Accounting Standards against IAS: Summary of Results. *Journal of International Accounting, Auditing & Taxation* 11, 77-90.

Sucher, Pat and Peter Kemp, 1998. Accounting and Auditing Reform in Belarus, *European Business Journal* 10(3): 141-147.

Tavernise, Sabrina. 2002. U.S. Auditors Find Things Are Different in Russia. *New York Times*, March 12, p. W1.

Tax Code of the Russian Federation, Provision #120.

Thornton, Judith. 1983. Twenty-Five Years of Soviet National Income Accounting: From Adjusted Factor Cost to Ultra-Adjusted Factor Cost. *ACES Bulletin* 25(3), 53-67.

Tolkushkin, A.V. 2001. *Istoriia nalogov v Rossii* (Moscow: Iurist), p. 264.

Transition Newsletter, World Bank Group [www.transitionnewsletter/]. Various issues.

Troika D ialog. 2 001. *C orporate Governance Principles*. R eview for W EF. [www.troika.ru]

Turk, Ivan & Neil Garrod. 1996. The Adaptation of International Accounting Rules: Lessons from Slovenia. In Neil Garrod & Stuart McLeay (Eds.), *Accounting in Transition: The Implications of Political and Economic Reform in Central Europe* (pp. 141-162) London & New York: Routledge.

USAID-Pragma Enterprise Development Project in Central Asia website www.casme.net/docs/newPDFeng/AR_FINALAAA%20(3).pdf

Vorushkin, Vladimir. 2001. IAS Benefits for Russian Enterprises: Managerial Issues. *International Center for Accounting Reform Newsletter*, March/April. [www.icar.ru/eng/newsletter/19.4.2001.html]

Vysokov, V. 2000. Center-invest: Banking in Russia using International Accounting Standards. *Euromoney*, Issue 377, September, p. 117.

Wagner, J., Stimpert, J., & Fubara, E. 1998. Board Composition and Organizational Performance: Two Studies of Insider/Outsider Effects. *Journal of Management Studies*, 35(5), 655-677.

Wallace, R.S. Olusegun. 1993. Development of Accounting Standards for Developing and Newly Industrialized Countries, *Research in Third World Accounting* 2: 121-165.

Williams, Thomas. 2001. Lawyers Pin Hopes on Reforms in Recovering Russia. *International Financial Law Review* 20:11 (November): 34.

World Bank Corporate Governance website www.worldbank.org/html/fpd/privatesector/cg/

Zelenka, Ivan, William Seal and Pat Sucher, 1996. The Emerging Institutional Framework of Accounting in the Czech and Slovak Republics, in Neil

Garrod and S tuart M cLeay, e ditors, *Ac counting in Transition: The Implications of Political and Economic Reform in Central Europe*, London and New York: Routledge 93-115.

Zhuravlev, Igor. 2001. International Accounting Qualification: Is It Supplementary Education or Necessity. *ICAR Newsletter* (July/August) www.icar.ru/eng/newsletter/19.8.2001.html

INDEX

178